The competent school manager

The competent school manager

Paul McCallion

London: The Stationery Office

Applications for reproduction should be made in writing to: the Contracts and Rights Manager, The Stationery Office Limited, St Crispins, Duke Street, Norwich NR3 1PD

The information contained in this publication is believed to be correct at the time of manufacture. Whilst care has been taken to ensure that the information is accurate, the publisher can accept no responsibility for any errors or omissions or for changes to the details given.

A CIP catalogue record for this book is available from the British Library
A Library of Congress CIP catalogue record has been applied for

First published 1998

ISBN 0 11 702317 5

Edited by Helen Baxter

Text designed and typeset by The Stationery Office

Cover designed by Richard Jones

Cover photograph supplied by Tuuliki Parker

Printed in Great Britain by The Stationery Office

J63108 C20 11/98 390617 19585

Contents

List of Tables

1: Basic principles of managing

Introduction

For the purposes of this book the term 'senior teacher' shall be used to describe all those teachers who have management responsibilities. This includes principals or head teachers, vice principals or deputy head teachers, department heads and any teacher who manages others including, of course, those who actually hold the job title Senior Teacher. The term will also be used interchangeably with that of manager.

Some of the ideas and concepts in this book are described in other books in this series. As certain basic concepts have applications in different settings, a decision had to be made as to whether the reader was referred elsewhere for a description of a concept or it was described at the point where it was relevant. The second approach was felt to be better. However, because of differences in context, the descriptions of ideas and concepts will differ or have a different emphasis while still being recognisably the same.

A manager or senior teacher could be defined as someone who has responsibility to lead and control the activities of others, in order to achieve the school's goals. Stated simply, a senior teacher achieves his aims through the activities of the people for whom he is responsible. In addition, most senior teachers have a responsibility to actually do certain tasks. Different levels of management tend to be defined by the amount of time spent 'doing' and the amount of time spent 'managing'.

Role of the senior teacher as manager

For many people new to a management role, this aspect of not doing but getting others to do is one of the most difficult. Often they will have been promoted on the basis of their ability to do the main tasks of their department. Once promoted, at least part of their time doing is replaced by management tasks. These are seldom as satisfactory as the 'doing' part of the job.

In a management position they will spend time communicating, helping others to do their job, planning, checking and co-ordinating the work of their department, with that of others. These are all essential tasks to the smooth running of the operation but are difficult to measure. The work of teachers and others who report to senior teachers can usually be easily and quickly measured.

To be effective as a senior teacher requires a very clear idea of what the role is and how to achieve it. The job needs to be defined placing it within the context of the school and the department. In particular, management tasks need to be differentiated. It is this part of the senior teacher's role which is this book's main focus.

Management tasks

A good starting point is to look at the job as it is currently done and define the key management tasks which are carried out For those who are using this book as preparation for taking on a management role, define the management tasks which current senior teachers in the school carry out. Management tasks are fairly easy to recognise and traditionally have been defined as those tasks which involve:

- planning

- organising

- motivating employees

- checking and controlling

- co-ordinating with other departments or schools

- delegating

- communicating.

A more modern view of management function emphasises the overall goal or vision and the actions necessary to achieve this.

This definition of management tasks on this model is as follows:

- A senior teacher defines the direction and general aims of the school, area or department for which she is responsible.

- She then defines the precise goals by which those general aims will be achieved.

- The senior teacher's next task is to gain the commitment or motivation of those working for her to achieve those goals.

- The senior teacher, with the help of her staff, then pursues those goals by whatever means necessary.

This model of management is comparable to the older model but emphasises the importance of establishing the initial direction or vision and of motivating people. In modern management terms, people are seen as the key resource.

The second model is, arguably a spin-off of the first with an increased emphasis on the overall vision and on people management. In a time of relative stability, when jobs and schools changed slowly, it was not necessary for an effective senior teacher to have a vision of where things were going – the direction was fairly clear. In more recent times, that has changed and successful schools and senior teachers are those who foresee and manage change.

It has been argued that, in the future, being a manager in any organisation will effectively mean managing change. If senior teachers see their role and function in terms only of the tasks they are required to do then sooner or later the school will change around them and they will be left behind. This is much less likely to happen if they see their role as fulfilling particular purposes of the school and their tasks as a means to that end. Stated simply, any school or senior teacher not actively managing change will eventually become the victim of it.

In most schools, there will be many changes that managers do not have the information to foresee. These changes will be imposed from above or be created by changes in technology or in the market place. In these circumstances, to cling to the traditional way of doing things might be understandable but will ultimately result in the person or even the whole school being bypassed.

Basic 'rules' of management

There are patterns to the situations, problems and behaviours that a senior teacher is likely to encounter. Most management situations are focused on changing what is happening, and usually trying to improve on the current circumstances. It is this that underlies what will be discussed both here and in the other chapters of the book.

The following set of approaches and principles is the key to good management practice, particularly management of change. It does not hold true in every possible set of circumstances but is generally applicable. In later chapters some themes mentioned here will recur as they are applied in working situations.

What is measured should improve

Managers are most likely to fail if they do not have up-to-date and accurate information on the important aspects of the operation. What is important will, however, change from time to time and a manager must be alert to those changes in emphasis. Measuring is not enough in itself, there must be an understanding of what constitutes both a good and a bad performance, and review and action on the measurements must occur.

Behaviour and reward

If a behaviour is rewarded, it is more likely to be repeated; if it obtains no reward it is more likely to stop.

The main difficulty here is often in identifying what the person or group finds rewarding and determining whether or not the senior teacher has any power to confer or withhold that. Most managers have more power than they recognise in respect of this. They have power over the working conditions of their people and they are able to give recognition for both good and bad work.

At a more general level, if the senior teacher is trying to eradicate undesirable behaviour then insight into the factors which the person finds rewarding from that behaviour can be helpful. Human behaviour is not a random event. It has causes and can be reinforced or discouraged.

People learn by doing

People retain very little of something they only hear. They are more likely to remember if it is actually seen. But if they are actually involved in doing they will remember and understand best of all.

First steps and the likelihood of success

Change is often principally about getting the process moving. If the first few steps are particularly difficult or unpopular, they will have an inordinately negative effect on attitudes to the whole process.

The converse is also true. Making change happen is often about overcoming the initial lethargy and resistance, building confidence and, therefore, momentum for change.

Non-verbal messages

Much of a manager's working time will be spent communicating with others. The figure of 70 percent is often quoted as the non-verbal part of the message. This figure is arguable, but there is general agreement that the non-verbal part of a communication is where most of the real meaning is carried. How people speak (their gestures, facial expressions and tone of voice), the context in which it is said and unexpected changes in their behaviour are all significant. This applies as much to the manager when passing a message to others as it does to anyone else.

What is done in the present

In managing change, what you do next month, next week or even tomorrow has less influence upon the likelihood of the change happening than what is done today and now.

Where this willingness to take immediate action is missing then it would be wise to be sceptical about the change actually happening. This applies as much to the manager as it does to anyone else. If a teacher or other staff member is not willing to do something now and today, then be realistic about the likelihood of that being different at some later point.

In planning change most people do not take into account the pressures that they will be under from unexpected sources in the future. Making change happen is about giving priority. This has little to do with being busy. It is busy people who find time to make change happen.

Motivation for change

Motivation for change is a function of four overlapping factors:

- fear, both of the change and of its consequences

- current habit and behaviour patterns

- wanting the change to happen or being convinced that it is necessary

- feeling in control of the change.

In order to motivate others to participate in change these factors must be addressed. Efforts to persuade people to participate will depend to a large degree on the ability of the manager to enthuse them on the one hand and to reassure them on the other about these four factors.

Owning the change

People are more likely to support change in those situations where they have a feeling of ownership. Where someone is following instructions he will usually do his best to achieve what is wanted. But when someone feels he owns the problem and the solution then he will do extra to find a solution. It is an observable aspect of human behaviour that we can be endlessly flexible and enthusiastic where there is a feeling of personal ownership.

This comes from feelings of being in control, having a strong say in decision making, benefiting directly from any good points and suffering from any negatives arising. If the person has invested time and effort or it has 'cost' him in some way, that too will add to the feelings of ownership. It is important, therefore, to try to get staff to feel they own what they do and the outcomes of their work.

People work better with deadlines and structure

A deadline can be the enemy of good quality since it can result in unnecessary rushing. However, without a deadline most people lack focus in achieving the important. If there is a choice between doing something that is urgent but not very important and something which is important but has no urgency most people choose the urgent task. Understanding this, a manager will consider putting deadlines on the important parts of the job even if they lack urgency.

The point can have even wider applications. Given a task to do that has no structure, most people will struggle to produce anything useful, unless they develop the parameters for themselves. Most good work is done under pressure and constraints. However, like the deadline, if these are too tight then the quality of what is done suffers.

A clear achievable target increases chances of success

We all need goals to focus on if we are to achieve our aims. The ability to translate a general aim, such as achieving good results or producing high-quality learning situations or reducing the amount of time wasted, into meaningful measurable goals is one of the most fundamental skills of management.

In-built resistance to change

People are creatures of habit. This shows itself in many ways, from how we carry out simple day-to-day activities such as eating, washing and dressing to the resistance which is demonstrated when attempts are made to change out-of-date laws or customs. A simple piece of behaviour has implications for many other activities. So even small changes can make us unsure and uncomfortable.

There is the added comfort factor that even if we are not coping well, familiarity at least gives the feeling that we understand what is happening. Change, however, raises concerns of the 'What will happen if?' kind.

These fears often have no foundation but the lack of previous experience of the new situation will make them seem very real. If a manager wants people to change there should be no surprise at their resistance even for what is perceived to be good for them.

Behaviour changes attitudes more often than attitudes change behaviour

There is often an assumption that if people's attitude is changed then a change in their behaviour will automatically follow. It comes as a surprise to many managers when they win the argument for change but the behaviour remains the same. There is a complicated interplay between behaviour and attitude with one influencing the other. However, most changes start with the change in behaviour and the attitudes fall in line after the event.

This goes against the view of human beings as rational people who weigh the evidence, make decisions and then act. Reality appears to be more cynical: people act and then justify their behaviour after the event to themselves and others. There is, however, a degree of truth in both analyses.

Not to take the cynical view into account will leave a manager disappointed and surprised at times. Changing behaviour and attitudes is often a complicated process which involves movement on both rather than one following the other. In planning changes at work a manager may be more successful if she tries first for a small change in behaviour and builds on that to change attitudes which, in turn, will lead on to more fundamental behaviour changes.

Management adaptability

Every situation and person is unique and one of the key skills in management is to be able to recognise when to deviate from what is the accepted answer.

Often it is our ability to recognise the patterns and similarities in events that gives us our understanding of them. The reverse is also true: recognising the unique features of an event and adapting the standard answer to take account of it is also important. From a motivational point of view, we all like to be treated as individuals and to have our own unique abilities, attributes and circumstances recognised. The manager who can make each person feel special and different has more opportunity of success in managing difficult situations.

2: Interview skills for managers

Introduction

Certain basic concepts are common to effective interviews of all kinds. These will be examined first and then the specifics of three particular types of interview will be examined in depth, these being:

- selection or recruitment interviews

- appraisal or assessment performance interviews

- disciplinary and grievance interviews.

The ability of an interviewer to ask questions, listen to the answers and respond to what is heard is the essence of good interviewing. Questioning technique will be looked at in some detail first, therefore. The content of this section is similar to that of other books in the series where counselling interviews are being examined.

Asking questions

The purpose of virtually all interviews is to find out information. Often, however, a manager may not want the interviewee to know the precise answer required, in case he gives that rather than his own views. In addition, most interviews are conducted in situations where the interviewee will want to present himself to best effect, where he may not want the interviewer to know the whole truth. Difficulties may be further compounded by having a nervous interviewee or one who does not cope well with a formal interview situation.

Skill in questioning will be critical to getting the best from what would be generally accepted as a difficult situation.

Open questions

Open questions could be defined as those which cannot be answered with a yes or a no (closed questions being those that can be answered in this way). They are sometimes called 'interrogative' questions. 'Interrogative' and 'interrogate' come from the same root word, and while it is not being suggested that interviews should become interrogations, it is worth reflecting that an interview and an interrogation share certain aspects. In both: the main means of finding out information is by asking questions; in addition, the interviewee may not want to give the full story; the interviewee may not know exactly what is being looked for in both.

Open questions usually begin with 'Who?', 'What?', 'Why?', 'When?', 'Where?', 'Which?' or 'How?' (Closed questions usually begin with 'Did you?', 'Could you?', 'Have you?', 'Are you?', or 'Will you?'.)

Leading questions

Be particularly careful of leading questions. They can take a number of forms but often begin with a statement such as 'Do you not think?', 'Have you considered?' or 'Why didn't you?'. Leading questions will seldom tell anything about the person's real views. The answer is usually based on what she believes the interviewer wants to hear.

Truth and genuine opinion

In all interview situations the interviewer wants to hear the truth or the interviewee's genuine opinions. Provocative remarks or questions may well result in the interviewee saying things he would not have wanted to say and for this reason some interviewers like to use them. But they often do not give a genuine picture of the person. Treat the interviewee with respect. The interviewer is not there to catch out the interviewee. So while questions may be probing or challenging, they should not be aimed at provoking the interviewee.

Short questions

If the content of the question is long then outline the main details and ask the question at the end. For example, 'I want to outline a set of circumstances to you ... How would you handle that?', as opposed to 'How would you handle a situation where?'. If the details are long then the interviewee will have forgotten the question by the time it is actually asked.

Situational questions

Situational questions can be a useful way to test knowledge and are of value, particularly in selection interviews.

Situational questions are those which ask the interviewee how she would handle a particular set or circumstances (or situation). Care is needed that the question will help the interviewee to demonstrate genuine understanding or knowledge. A simple test of memory or the ability to recite a procedure will not really tell you much about what the person would actually do if the situation arose.

Fairness is another important point. If there are internal and external candidates at a selection interview, a situational question could favour the internal candidates, particularly if it is asking them to repeat the organisation's procedures or is based on an incident that has actually happened.

'Double-barrelled' questions

These are questions which are really two questions, for example, 'What are the most important issues in ... and how do you ensure that they are properly addressed?'. If there are two questions, ask the first, listen to the answer and then ask the second. Asking the two together makes it more difficult for the interviewee who is genuinely trying to answer the question. It is likely that he will answer one part and forget the other, or try to answer both together and actually answer neither very satisfactorily.

For the less genuine interviewee, it may let him 'off the hook'. That person can answer the part that he wants to and ignore the part that he is uncomfortable with. It also gives the opportunity to talk around both questions without really answering either, while appearing to answer both.

Putting the candidate at ease

Some time should be spent at the start of interviewing putting the candidate at her ease. Even in a disciplinary interview (and perhaps particularly so) this is important. It can be done in a number of ways:

- Strike up a casual conversation at the start about the weather, the person's journey to the interview, work being done that day or other matters of interest.

- Give the interviewee an outline of the purpose and structure of the interview.

- Introduce those present, where this is appropriate.

- Tell the interviewee to relax or not to be nervous. This at least demonstrates that the purpose is not to catch the person out but to get the best from him in a selection interview, to get the whole truth about what happened in a disciplinary interview and to get as much as possible of a positive nature from an appraisal interview.

- A humorous remark (not usually advisable in disciplinary interviews). This can break the ice and help the person to settle at the start of the interview. Humour should not be at the expense of the interviewee.

Expected answers

Interviewers who have not thought through the answers that are expected find it difficult to recognise and respond to an inadequate or vague answer.

Follow-up questions

The real skill in asking questions is not in the ability to ask a good initial question, important as this is; it is in the interviewer's response to the answer.

Sometimes an unsatisfactory response is followed by the interviewer asking 'Is there anything else you would do?' or 'What other factors would you take into account?'. In other words, a question where the interviewer is simply asking for more. It must be assumed that the interviewee has given her best. Asking for more is unlikely to produce a better response. It is more likely to become a guessing game.

It is better to take a point from the interviewee's answer and ask a further open question on that. For example, 'Why do you feel it is important to?', 'When would you involve?' or 'You mentioned ... What experience do you have of that?'.

Listen for vague statements or ones which do not give detail and ask follow-up questions to find out more information. For example, 'You said that you would ... What experience have you actually had of doing this?' or 'You mentioned good communication as being important. What do you mean by "good communication"?'.

Watch the interviewee as well as listening

Body language does not tell what the other person is thinking, but a change in facial expression or posture at a critical moment, an over-reaction to a question or an air of defensiveness when discussing certain issues can all indicate an area where more questions should be asked.

Confidence of candidate

Interviews are aimed at obtaining the truth so making the interviewee feel relaxed and confident is important. The ability to ask probing or challenging questions that find out precise detail and put the candidate under pressure has already been emphasised. However, procedures which are aimed at humiliating the interviewee or aggressive questioning techniques should have no place in the interview process. Challenging questions aimed at clarifying areas of vagueness and drawing further information from a withdrawn or nervous interviewee are, however, important skills for the interviewer.

Interest in the interviewee's answers

Interviewers who indicate that they want to hear more are more likely to get satis factory responses.

Changing tone and atmosphere

The ability to change the tone and atmosphere of an interview is another critical skill. Knowing when an interview is so relaxed that the interviewer is not getting what is needed or when it has become so challenging that the interviewee feels defensive and then being able to respond to that is a key skill. It is for this reason that most interviews are conducted by more than one person, as there will then always be at least one person who can 'sit back' and see what is going on and respond appropriately.

Selection interviews

The choice of the right people is among the most important decisions a manager will make. Selection decisions will have a significant effect on interviewees, school and department alike and on the senior teacher who will be the successful candidate's manager. The costs of making the wrong decisions can be very high both in monetary terms and in the loss of productive work.

Stated in terms of the costs of buying the wrong equipment, decisions about who to employ or promote will usually be higher in monetary terms and have a bigger effect on an organisation's ability to do its work. Good selection interviewing is at least as important as spending time selecting the right piece of machinery or equipment.

Choosing the right person has other implications. Time and costs of training, the efficiency of those who work with the person and the school's compliance with employment law are all related issues. Perhaps the best reason for putting time and effort into this process is the moral one that fairness dictates that the most suitable person should get the job. That is the best outcome for both applicants and the school.

The essence of good selection is:

• Have a clear idea of what the school wants the person to do.

• Think through the blend of experience, qualifications and qualities which the successful applicant should have.

• Advertise in such a manner as to attract enough suitable candidates to make a selection.

• Select on the basis of suitability.

• Create a selection process rigorous enough to allow the best candidate to demonstrate his suitability. It must also be fair to all candidates and should not be the means by which those selecting humiliate or mistreat the candidates.

There are limitations to the interview as the means of selecting employees. All managers can be swayed by a good presentation or put off by a poor presentation. If presentation skills are critical to doing the job then this is reasonable. Where this is not the case, then the influence of this aspect is worrying.

There are others methods of aiding selection such as the use of psychometric tests or assessment techniques which require the candidates to demonstrate the skills needed for the job. For example, personality tests, practical exercises and assessment of skill in a relevant area are commonly used. There are other techniques, some of which are of more dubious value. Any additional techniques used should:

- have a clear relationship to the requirements for the job

- be based solidly on objective fact about their effectiveness

- be properly administered

- ensure that the requirements placed on the candidates are reasonable and fair.

If these criteria are adhered to then such techniques can be a valuable aid to good selection. Techniques which rely on less well-validated methods of selection are more likely to confuse the situation.

This book is concerned with the skills needed by senior teachers or managers and it is through interviewing that most schools will make selection decisions even if they use other techniques as supporting evidence.

Preparation for selection interview

Good interviewing depends on good preparation. If interviewers do not know what they are looking for from an interview, then they have very little hope of appointing the right candidate. Two pieces of preparation are very important in this: the job description and the personnel specification.

These are sometimes called by other names and in some schools it has been common to combine the two into a single document. The format of these documents and their names are less important than that the information is prepared in some manner. The job description refers to the duties and responsibilities the post holder will carry out. The personnel specification refers to qualifications, experience and / or the abilities and qualities which the successful applicant should have.

Preparation should also include a check on the school's procedures and approaches to filling vacancies. Where schools are criticised by external bodies for being unfair or not treating all candidates equally, it is often a failure in this respect. Any outside body investigating a selection decision will want to know first, if procedures exist and second, if they were followed. These two are perceived as being important in making the right decisions and in being able to demonstrate that the right decisions have been made.

This point extends through all the records and administration systems of the selection process. However, it should be emphasised that this should not be the main motivating factor in preparation and record keeping. Selecting the right people for the right jobs should be motivation enough.

Drafting a job description

There are a number of accepted formats for a job description, but for simplicity's sake one will be presented here. There is no right format or content and it may be necessary from time to time to review its structure to reflect the needs of a particular job. Broadly speaking there are two main types of job description.

The first is sometimes called the open or dynamic style. This seeks to outline general, overall responsibilities with the clear implication that the post holder will have to do whatever is necessary to meet those responsibilities. In this type, a series of goals is often defined along with the timescale. These goals and the associated responsibilities will be changed and redefined from time to time. This style is particularly suitable in jobs where the role has to be created by the post holder. In start-up situations and in fast changing environments where foretelling the shape of the job is going to be difficult, this approach has value. However, it tends to suit only a minority of situations.

The other type, and the one we shall examine more closely in this section, is where the job description seeks to define, in some detail, what is expected from the person, how she is expected to do the job, and her duties and responsibilities are described. Even with this type of job description there has to be some flexibility. Jobs do not remain the same and, however detailed, a job description will never cover everything the post holder is expected to do.

In order to define any job it must be placed within the context of the school and the department in which the person works. The first step, therefore, is to define the purposes, since from the purposes, the other elements of the job description can be developed.

Purposes

These can be difficult to define. When interviewers try to state the purposes of a job, they often focus on the actual activities that the person carries out. For example, the purposes of a sales assistant's job could be defined as 'selling'. But this is just a description of the activities the person carries out. The purposes of the sales assistant's job could be more properly defined as enabling the organisation to present its products and services in a professional manner. Or to enable customers to pay for the goods or services they wish to purchase. In order to achieve those purposes the sales assistant sells goods or operates a cash register.

The difference may seem a small one but this example of purposes describes two different kinds of sales assistant. In the first, the duties of the sales assistant will be reflected in a more positive selling role. The second could describe a check-out operator in a supermarket. This sales assistant helps the customers to buy but does not usually attempt to sell anything to them.

This division between purposes and activities becomes even more important at management level. If managers only define their jobs in terms of its activities, then aims will extend no further than carrying those activities out to the best of their ability. If they can see beyond the activities to the purposes then they will be much more flexible in adapting to changes.

The easiest way to ensure that managers are stating purposes rather than activities is by asking the question 'Why do we do that?'.

To take another example: why does a typist type? The reasons might be, for example, in order that the written communication from the department is both legible and professional. Why does the typist ensure that written communications are both legible and professional? Perhaps the answer here is to ensure that the written communications are understood and taken seriously. At this point the definition has moved beyond the responsibility of most typists. The purposes of the typist's job, therefore, relate to presentation and once you have gone beyond that point the next set of purposes relates to the person who gives the work to the typist. The purposes of the typist's job have therefore been defined.

The same can be applied to any job. Define the activity. Ask 'Why do they do that?'. Keep asking that same question until the level of responsibility goes beyond the individual, to the person whom she reports to. At that point the purposes of the job have almost certainly been defined. The same process can be applied to a department or whole school, and needs to be done for every activity.

Duties and responsibilities

Once the purposes have been defined the next step is to define the means by which those purposes are achieved. This is a definition of activities and areas of responsibility and this is usually a fairly straightforward exercise since it is a statement of what the person actually does.

The writing style of this section should be simple and clear. If the employee is expected to 'do', then it is usually better if it is written in a style that implies action rather than just responsibility. For example, 'Operate the cash register accurately', rather than 'Has responsibility for the operation of the cash register in an accurate manner'. They both mean the same, broadly speaking, but the second is a less active statement of what is essentially an activity. If the person does not have to do but ensure that something is done then the 'has responsibility for' approach is more appropriate.

Some statement indicating that the list is not exhaustive and that the person may be asked to do other things from time to time is important. Many people perceive a job description to be the same as a contract, when the two are, in fact, separate documents. Contracts are fixed and can only be changed with negotiation. Job descriptions are more open and while significant changes need to be negotiated there will always be some movement and change in jobs. Some indication of this is needed in a job description.

Key tasks

When developing a job description, it is important that it is clear which are the key duties and responsibilities. In any job there will be a range of tasks, some of which are done frequently, some of which are critical to the job outcomes and some of which are infrequent and / or relatively unimportant. There are a number of ways of highlighting the most important group.

Probably the simplest way is to define the key tasks. These are the duties and / or responsibilities where the post holder's performance is judged. This is usually written as the section following the duties and responsibilities and is simply a repetition of the principal tasks and responsibilities.

An alternative approach is to highlight the key tasks in the main body of the duties and responsibilities section. A third approach could be to define the amount of time to be spent on each area, the theory being that the more important aspects should attract the largest amount of time. In reality, however, the relationship between the amount of time and importance is often only a very general one. The recommended approach is, therefore, to define the key tasks.

Limits of responsibility

These are relatively straightforward. The basic questions are:

- How far is the post holder allowed to go before he must consult someone else?

- What decisions cannot be taken by the post holder?

- When must the post holder ask permission or approval from the line manager or someone else?

Limits of authority can apply to virtually any duties or responsibilities. The most common areas include:

- spending

- responsibility for disciplinary matters

- decision-making powers

- requirements to consult or inform

- authority to change policy in specific circumstances

- authority to give instructions and / or directions to others.

Strictly speaking each of the duties and responsibilities should have its own authority limit. In reality, most jobs have three or four strictly defined limits to authority and the rest are implied.

One format for a job description can be seen in Table 2.1.

Table 2.1 Sample job description format

JOB TITLE

DEPARTMENT   REPORTS TO

RESPONSIBLE FOR

MAIN PURPOSES OF POST

1

2

3

DUTIES AND RESPONSIBILITIES

1

2

3

4

5

6

7

8

9

10

11

12

KEY TASKS

1

2

3

LIMITS OF AUTHORITY

1

2

3

Specifying criteria for selection

This is usually referred to as the employee specification or the personnel specification. It is a definition of the blend of qualifications, experience, abilities, qualities and attributes that interviewers hope the post holder will have. As with the job description, there are a number of different formats, all of which have merit.

It is usual for the personnel specification to be divided into categories. These help interviewers to think through in some detail the precise requirements that they have. Like the job description, these must be defined in advance to have any real hope of selecting the most suitable candidate.

The format suggested here is by no means the only effective way. However, it does help to focus on a range of factors under different category headings.

The personnel specification is used at two main points in the selection process. At shortlisting stage, it is used to reduce the number of candidates to a manageable number to interview. At interview, it becomes the basis on which the final decision is made. In a professionally run selection process, it should be possible for someone coming after the event, to trace through from the job description and the range of duties and responsibilities defined, to the requirements developed from that in the personnel specification, and finally on to the decisions as to who was shortlisted, interviewed, selected and rejected. The reasons for the decisions made at each stage should be clear.

In defining requirements for the candidates, it is useful to think in terms of what is essential for the post holder to have and what is desirable. The personnel specification will likewise be written in this way. This will give some flexibility to decision making. At this stage interviewers will not know what applications will be received. Desirable criteria will allow them to tighten or loosen the requirements depending on the response to the advertisement.

Strictly speaking all those who meet the essential requirements should be interviewed and the final decision should be based on the ability of the interviewees to meet the desirable criteria. In many circumstances, this will be difficult to achieve. So shortlisting often consists of progressively tightening the criteria towards those defined as desirable, while still having a reasonable range of candidates to interview.

Essential criteria are precisely that: essential to do the job as defined. If a candidate does not meet the essential criteria then she should not progress any further. With some criteria that may not be possible to ascertain until the candidate has been called for interview. If none of the candidates meets the essential criteria then none of them would be appointed. The school would either re-advertise or look again at the job description and, therefore, the personnel specification.

Most personnel specifications have very few essential and a large number of desirable criteria. While interviewers would want the post holder to meet all the requirements, in reality most jobs could be held satisfactorily by someone who did not meet them all in every respect.

A further useful category to consider is whether there are any criteria which would make a candidate less suitable. It is usually better if these are then stated in the positive. For example, the criterion could be that candidates should have a broad range of experience (providing interviewers define what they mean by that) rather than stating that restricted experience would make a candidate less suitable. So while the negatives may not appear on the personnel specification, it can be helpful to think in terms of those things which would make a candidate less suitable or would disqualify her.

A further consideration, when defining the personnel specification, is the notion of equivalence. The most obvious example of this is in qualifications. In defining a qualification, particularly one which is essential, it is important to think through whether there are other ways in which candidates can meet the requirements. A phrase stating that the equivalent will be accepted is often sufficient.

The problem can be more difficult to address if the criteria relate to personality factors. Interviewers may have a clear idea about the type of person needed to do the job. However, it is very possible that a different approach and personality could be equally effective.

The issue of equality of opportunity is very relevant here. In a job that has been traditionally carried out only by men or women, there may be an accepted approach which would favour the sex which has traditionally done the work. That does not mean that members of the other sex could not do an equally good or even better job by approaching it in another way. Often there is a bias towards the way the current post holder does the job. Again, if that person is particularly successful in the post it could be difficult to conceive of the job being done successfully in any other way.

In most cases this problem can be avoided by looking again at the job description and thinking through the implications of the duties and responsibilities for the characteristics of the future post holder. It is important not to include irrelevant criteria simply because they have been traditionally included or because it is fashionable to ask for them. Criteria should genuinely help choose the right person to carry out the duties and responsibilities. Others only restrict the choice unnecessarily or introduce arbitrary constraints.

Question the value of all criteria and examine whether or not there are alternatives. Be particularly careful of criteria which directly or indirectly favour males or females or one group over any other. If the criterion is genuinely needed for the job then it may be acceptable. If in doubt it is better to contact one of the equality bodies for advice.

As already stated there are many ways of categorising the criteria of a personnel specification. The following gives a useful and comprehensive list for most jobs.

Physical characteristics

Physical requirements are, usually, more obvious in jobs which have definite physical aspect to them. However, many jobs have some physical requirements, for example good vision, a height requirement, a good telephone voice, neatness or good grooming. As with all criteria, the duties and responsibilities must be examined closely.

Colour blindness is an example of a criterion which could make someone less suitable. This could be re-stated in the positive as 'good colour vision'. Also included in this category can be a reference to the health or sickness record of the post holder. Age is sometimes included here, either a minimum or maximum age. While, at the time of writing, there are no legal penalties for discriminating on the basis of age, it is normally an irrelevance when used.

Employers often want an older person because of the experience he would have. Or want a younger person because he will be more willing to move location or to learn. If these are relevant, then they are the real criteria (i.e. experience, willingness to move location or ability / willingness to learn). It would be better to think what lies behind the criterion of age and include that in the personnel specification rather than making generalised assumptions about younger or older people.

If there are no significant physical requirements then do not include them just to fill a space. A frivolous criterion will devalue the whole exercise.

Education

These are probably the most straightforward to define. As already stated be careful not to define a single characteristic when there are other possible equivalents. The words 'or equivalent' after the qualification will usually be sufficient.

One danger with qualifications is that because they tend to be factual and easy to define they are often used as the means artificially to reduce the number of suitable applicants. This is done by asking for higher qualifications than the job needs. If a better qualified person will do the job better, then this is a reasonable approach. However, if, once the minimum educational standard has been achieved, additional qualifications do not make a better employee, then choice is being unnecessarily restricted.

The problem can be a serious one where there are a large number of candidates for a small number of jobs and a full selection procedure will be unnecessarily time consuming. It would be better, however, if relevant criteria were used to reduce the numbers rather than artificial ones.

The reverse situation can also arise. Sometimes individuals are excluded for being too well-qualified. The argument for this normally runs that the better qualified candidate is really looking for something better, will not settle easily to work beneath her ability level and it is better not to employ her in the first place. There is actually little evidence that this is true. Furthermore, if the school is likely to have a requirement for internal candidates for promoted posts in the future then it is better to have some people who will be likely to want and be able to fill these positions.

Conversely, before employing someone who is clearly over-qualified for a job it would be better to ascertain that she is aware and willing to accept the repetitive aspects of the work and try to get some indication of her willingness to stay with the job.

Experience

As with education, experience is usually relatively easy to define. The requirement for experience has changed in recent years as a result of changes in work practices and technology. As a result, sometimes the term 'recent experience' is used in personnel specifications. As before, interviewers should question what this means: is it experience of new technology, processes or working practices? Whatever it is, it is probably better that these be defined rather than using a term like 'recent' without explanation.

Personality

Sometimes this category is defined as social skills and personal qualities. It is usually a reference to the ability of people with different personal attributes to do the job. Some jobs require leadership, some teamwork. Others require the person to be able to communicate with groups, while yet others require the post holder to work on his own initiative. Other criteria include patience, punctuality, assertiveness, being able to work under pressure and honesty.

The tendency with this category is to ask for so many characteristics that no one could possibly have them all. Try to be realistic about what is genuinely needed and include only those. If most of the existing post holders do not have the characteristic but are still satisfactory in the job then why is it being asked for from the new person?

The other difficulty that relates to this category is how to ascertain whether or not the person has the characteristic. Interviews are not normal situations for most people. So it will be unlikely that interviewers will be able to make a genuine judgement about the person from their performance at interview alone. Personality tests and practical exercises are alternative approaches. However, even without these it is possible to make some judgements about the candidates.

The person's interests and hobbies will give some indication of what the person is like. Situational questions will also give some insight into how the individual works with others. Probing questions about the candidate's past experience and what he perceives to be his achievements will also help. Some aspects of his background will also be instructive. Suppose, for example, interviewers were seeking 'honesty' as an attribute: a candidate who had been given responsibility for something which required a good deal of honesty and has held that responsibility over a long period has demonstrated evidence of honesty.

Special skills and circumstances

These criteria are, to some degree, a catch-all for aspects not covered in the other categories. Special skills can cover a wide range of criteria depending on the post. Some posts, of course, may have no special skills or special knowledge associated with them.

'Circumstances' refers to any special aspects relating to the job which will affect the post holder's life beyond her work. The ability to move location at short notice would be one example. Shift work or the possibility of being called out outside of normal working hours would be others, as would having own transport or a driving licence.

Criteria relating to circumstances could be expressed as an ability to work in a particular way or a willingness to meet the requirements of the work.

Summary

This is a repeat of the key criteria from the other categories. The summary is used for the advertisement. The interviewers will then have both what the interviewees have been told are the criteria and the full set of criteria in one document.

The category within which a particular criterion is placed is less important than having the criterion included. It is on the following that attention should be focused:

- Will the criterion ensure that the post holder is able to do his job?

- If not, will it make it more or less likely that he will do the job better?

- If it does, why is that?

- Has the real criterion been defined or an associated factor?

- Does the criterion, as defined, make it more or less likely that a man, a woman or member of minority group will be selected?

- If it does have a direct or indirect bias, is this criterion a fundamental part of the job or is it there because of a preconception about how the job should be done?

As with the job description, be careful about taking a previously written document and reusing that. Jobs and requirements do change. The last ten years, in particular, have seen major changes in both technology and working practices. The idea of having a set job description and personnel specification (Table 2.2.) which is dusted down every time it is needed is no longer practical. Also be careful of changing such documents just for the sake of it.

The job description and personnel specification are key documents. If they are right, selection will usually still be difficult. If they are wrong then it is likely that either the wrong candidate will be selected, or it will be difficult to demonstrate why the most suitable candidate failed to be indicated as that. Many of the problems interviewers have judging who is the most suitable candidate or being taken in by a very articulate candidate come back to a failure to take these two documents seriously.

Table 2.2. Sample personnel specification

POST

DEPARTMENT

CATEGORY	ESSENTIAL	DESIRABLE
PHYSICAL CHARACTERISTICS		
EDUCATION		
EXPERIENCE		
PERSONALITY		
SPECIAL SKILLS AND CIRCUMSTANCES		
SUMMARY		

Developing questions

The basic principles underlying the development of questions were defined earlier in this chapter. Sample questions are given later for each category of the personnel specification. These should not be looked on as the only or best questions – that can only be decided in the knowledge of the specific job and its requirements.

Interviewers should always have a set of prepared questions for interview. This ensures fairness for all candidates. Equally an interview panel should have the flexibility to be able to follow through on a specific aspect with any candidate. This could be something arising out of her application form, previous experience or as a result of a point made by the candidate. Some interviewers believe that fairness can only be maintained by asking all the candidates precisely the same questions and not deviating from that set in any way. This is neither necessary nor is it good practice.

A prepared set of questions will ensure that all candidates are given the opportunity to talk about the same areas. Flexibility in following up specific aspects allows the individual candidate to demonstrate her unique experience or abilities and allows the interviewers to clarify and examine precise aspects of each candidate's application.

While the questions will depend on the criteria defined the following set may be useful. The order given is that in which the criteria appear on the personnel specification. However, questions will probably not be asked in this order. Usually after the initial question the areas of experience and education are examined.

The initial question should be focused on the job being applied for. It should also be relatively easy to answer, in order to get the candidate talking. For example:

- What was it about this post that attracted you to it?

- What, in your opinion, are the qualities needed for this job?

- What do you know about the school?

An interviewer may wish to vary the wording in these or any of the subsequent questions suggested. Choose questions which are suitable to the criteria defined on the personnel specification.

Physical characteristics

- How many days sick leave have you had in the last year?

- What importance do you place on good personal appearance?

- This post will require you to ...What problems will that cause you?

- How would you ensure that your appearance matched the requirements of the job?

- What serious illnesses or health problems have you had?

- What in your opinion are the physical requirements for this job? How do you meet those requirements? (This is second or follow-up question. The two questions should not be asked together.)

Education

- What were your favourite subjects in school? What was it about those that you particularly liked?

- What school subjects did you not like? What was it about them that you disliked?

- How has education (or a particular qualification) helped you to do your job better?

- What methods of study did you use in approaching examinations? (Usually only suitable for those with qualifications from further or higher education.)

- What are your future intentions concerning education?

- How did your job training help you to do your job better?

- If you were asked to review the education and training you received and make recommendations for the training of future employees, what changes would you suggest?

- What regrets do you have about your education?

- How do you ensure that your knowledge is kept up to date?

- What training or education have you participated in in the last three years? How did it help you to do your job better?

Experience

- How has your experience to date prepared you for the post you are now applying for?

- What are the main duties and responsibilities of your present job?

- Describe a difficult situation which you have had to handle in your current post.

- What were your reasons for wanting to leave ... (a previous post)?

- What are your reasons for wanting to leave your present post?

- Which job did you enjoy most? What was it that made it enjoyable?

- What do you enjoy most about your present job?

- Who has had the most influence on you during your working life? What difference did that influence make to you? Why did they have such influence on you?

Personality

- How would you describe your personality?

- What interests do you have outside work? / What do you do in your spare time?

- What are your ambitions? How will this post help you meet those ambitions?

- What are the most important factors in your motivation at work?

- What do you understand by the term 'teamwork'?

- Why is it important to work co-operatively with others?

- What are the signs of low morale in a department? (Question suitable for management and supervisory jobs.)

- How do you cope with stress at work?

- How would you cope with having to carry out disciplinary actions with one of your former colleagues? (Question suitable for internal candidate applying for management or supervisory position.)

- How important in doing the job is good communication?

In addition, a range of situational questions will be useful in this context. Good situational questions will have a clash of priorities in them. For example, how to handle a complaint about another member of staff is relatively straightforward, there will probably be a procedure. How the person would handle a complaint that he did not believe to be true is a much better question. Equally, how to provide good-quality teaching is a relatively straightforward question but balancing the needs of the better and less able pupils within a group will tell more about the interviewee's attitudes and approach.

Situational questions are not there to catch the candidate out. Their purpose is to introduce some of the genuinely difficult situations that will arise in the job and get a feeling for how the person will respond to them. How he will actually respond may be entirely different and is an area you are unlikely to be able to judge at interview.

Special skills and circumstances

- What experience do you have of ... (a special skill)?

- You will have to work irregular hours what problems will this cause you? (If the hours are unusual then you may want to investigate whether someone who has not worked this pattern before understands what the implications are.)

- How will you travel between home and work? (If there are not likely to be problems, this question may not be relevant.)

- How would you cope with requests to work extra hours at short notice?

Interviewers should be careful in asking questions about 'circumstances' that their preconceptions do not lead them into making assumptions about different groups. For example, that a married woman with children will not want to work certain hours or shifts or that she will have childcare problems. It should be assumed that if the candidate has had advance knowledge of the hours and conditions and still wants to be considered, then she believes that they can be met.

Conversely it is entirely reasonable, where there has been difficulty with particular working patterns or where the location raises certain problems, that interviewers satisfy themselves that candidates have understood the implications of taking on the job. This is particularly the case where that person has until now not had to face these issues.

Interviewers should ask themselves if they would ask the same question from a man / woman / member of another ethnic group. One specific situation is worth noting here. Sometimes employers define availability as being a criterion for selecting staff. There is usually no problem with this but it should not apply in the case of a pregnant woman. If the reason why the candidate is not available is that she is pregnant and if, other things being equal, she is most suitable candidate, then she should not be rejected for the post.

Even though her pregnancy makes her unavailable, it is discriminatory because pregnancy only affects women. To reject a candidate for that reason is to discriminate on the grounds of the gender of the candidate. Interviewers are treating that candidate less favourably than they would a man (that applies also even where the selected candidate is a woman).

Questions exercise

The following is a series of difficult selection situations. The task is to decide how to handle each one and what questions to ask. For each, outline three possible questions. To complete the exercise it might be useful to have a particular job in mind, as this will help in framing the questions. This exercise can be done individually but is probably best done as a discussion exercise.

A You are interviewing for a post which will require strong interpersonal skills. You know that not all candidates will display these at interview, even though they may display them when they come to do the job. What questions could you ask that would help to assess personality factors of this kind?

B In the post you are interviewing for, a broad range of relevant experience has been defined as a criterion. All the interviewees have a number of years of appropriate experience. However, you believe that the working experience of some of them is restricted (e.g. one year's experience repeated ten times rather than ten years' experience). What questions would help you to ascertain the breadth of the candidates' experience?

C You have asked the interviewee why he wishes to leave his present job. The person replies that the reasons are associated with personal relationships and he does not wish to discuss them further. In every other respect, this person is the most suitable for the post. However, this answer has raised doubts in your mind about the ability of the candidate to work co-operatively with others (a defined criterion for the post). What follow-up questions could you ask in this situation?

D The post requires the employee to work outside normal school hours at quite short notice. There would also be late night and weekend work from time to time. The interviewee has mentioned in passing that she has three young children. What questions should / can you ask to ensure that she will meet the requirements of the post?

E The person you are interviewing comes from a similar school to yours. You have been told that this person is reasonably good at his job but is difficult to work with. These reports are only rumour but are probably accurate. Because of changes which are being currently introduced, teamwork will be a critical part of the job. On paper, this person has the best qualifications and experience. However, if the reports are true the interviewee would be totally unsuitable. What questions could you ask which would help you clarify the suitability of this candidate?

Comments

These comments are meant as general guidance only. Each situation will have unique features which must be taken into account. This is intended to outline the main points that should be considered. For this reason, specific questions have not been suggested. In the real situation, interviewers must also take into account the likely impact of any questions asked in the light of equality of opportunity and other similar issues.

In situation **A**, the problem is a common one. There are a number of ways of judging personality factors (for example, a good personality test, properly administered and scored can give high-quality information). In reality, it is very difficult to judge factors of this kind before the person has worked in the job for some time. Very few selection processes allow this to happen. Judging personality purely from interview performance is not easy. But interviewers can get some insight.

Questions about the person's spare time activities can give insight into personality. What the person has enjoyed about previous jobs or disliked about them might help also. Another common approach is to ask situational questions. That is, how would the person handle a difficult situation of an interpersonal kind. An alternative to this would be to ask him to identify a difficult interpersonal situation that he has handled in the current job and to describe his handling of that.

Situation **B** highlights another set of problems. Length of time doing a job is often a very poor indicator of breadth of experience. Probing or challenging questions are of value here. Ask interviewees for examples of what they have done and the variety of experiences that they have had. A question on the candidate's beliefs about the type of experience necessary to do the job with a follow up on how she measures up to that could also be useful.

The most important aspect of situation B, however, is that the interviewers are very clear about the type and range of experience that they believe is important and that the questions asked are directed towards ascertaining how well the interviewees meet those requirements. Good definition of criteria at the personnel specification stage is what is important. So 'a broad range of experience' needs to be much better defined.

The main concern about situation **C** for most interviewers is whether they can ask any questions at all. The difficulty is that when the interviewee has made a statement like this interviewers will not know what lies behind it and will probably start making assumptions. Most of these assumptions will be not help the interviewee get the job.

It is difficult to give an absolute answer to this situation – an interviewer would have to judge the circumstances at the time. In most cases it would probably be better to pursue the matter further. There are a number of questions possible.

The key aspect is that it is reasonable to ask how a person will cope in the job being applied for. But as the person has said that he do not wish to discuss the details of the matter the interviewer must respect his right to privacy. It is only fair, however, to point out to the interviewee problems if he insists on this and how it affects the panel's judgement of his suitability. This situation is made particularly difficult by the fact that the interviewee is the most suitable in every other respect.

Situation **D** is probably the most straightforward of all. The fact that the interviewee is a woman and has young children is irrelevant. It would be usual to ask any candidate for a job how they will cope with unusual hours or other difficulties that were different from normal. The simple rule of thumb is that you should not ask someone a question that you would not in similar circumstances ask a member of the opposite sex or a member of another racial, national, regional, religious or political group. In other words, you should not make assumptions about the behaviour or problems that a person might have because she is or is not a member of a particular group.

Situation **E** highlights the problem of introducing information from outside the selection process. As the scenario is written, it would seem that the information you have is so vague as to be useless. If the candidate is the best, then, other things being equal, it would be hard to turn the person down on the basis of this.

If teamwork is important then this should be reflected in questioning in any case. What experience do the interviewees have of teamwork? What problems have the interviewees experienced working in teams? How would the interviewees cope with interpersonal conflict within teams? How they would react in a situation where they could not get on with another or other members of the team? What are the signs of good teamwork? What could be done if the signs of good teamwork were not present in a team that the person was working in?

These are all types of question that could be asked of any interviewee. More specific questions on the team the person is currently a member of could be more difficult because of the confidentiality aspect but may be admissible in some circumstances.

Selection administration

There are a number of administrative steps which are needed following interview. The principal of these is writing to inform successful and unsuccessful candidates of the outcome. In addition, the panel may wish to seek references. However, the most important part of administration for many interviewers relates to the notes they keep.

These notes have their most obvious use should decisions be questioned or should a complaint be taken out by a candidate with one of the bodies with responsibility for fairness. In such circumstances, notes taken at the time or immediately after the interview may be admissible as evidence. Notes written up some time afterwards will almost certainly not be admitted. If there are no notes then interviewers will have to rely on memory – and many tribunal cases are heard many months and sometimes years after the selection was made.

More important than this, the act of committing thoughts to writing will force interviewers to think through the reasons for decisions. They are more likely to make better decisions as a result. Notes at interview will be of two kinds:

- Comments written during the interview reflecting how the interviewer feels the person has answered the questions.

- A record of the decisions that were taken and why they were taken. For example, there might be more than one suitable candidate. Notes would indicate why the panel decided which of those would be offered the job and why. Another example might be that during the interview an individual interviewer felt that one of the interviewees answered a question well or badly. Following discussion with other interviewers she might have changed her opinion. The notes would reflect that.

Be careful of making notes about irrelevant issues. It will be assumed that if an interviewer has recorded something in writing that it was part of the decision-making process.

A standard form for interview assessment is of value. This should reflect the categories on the personnel specification. A grading system, while not essential, can be helpful. One approach is to weight the value of each factor. For example, for one particular job, qualifications might get a 50 percent rating, personality 30 percent, experience 10 percent, physical factors 5 percent and special skills and circumstances, 5 percent also. In this case, qualifications would be marked out of 50, personality out of 30, and so on. In this way when all the scores were added up the person with the highest score would be offered the job.

In some jobs weighting the various factors may not be possible. Strength in one area may cancel out weakness in another. An alternative, therefore, is to score each factor independently. Be careful, however, that this cannot become the subject of a simple addition by someone else afterwards. Scoring each factor out of the same total when they are not all of equal value can throw up anomalies. A system that is graded by letters can avoid problems caused by this.

A sample interview assessment record is given in Table 2.3. This has the value of being a single page record. It may not seem an important point but when an interviewer is assessing a large number of interviewees, being able to see all the comments on one candidate on a single page simplifies the task. The decision and reasons section is very important where there is more than one suitable candidate.

All interviewers should complete their own interview assessment record. The minimum number to conduct interviews is two (schools and local education authorities will virtually always have their own minimum numbers which will be higher than this). This number is set for the protection of interviewers. If there is a dispute afterwards about what was said or done then having more than one person will help to demonstrate fairness. More important, different people will view answers to questions and the interviewee's conduct in the interview in different ways. Having other views will make the assessment a more accurate one. In addition, it takes the pressure off interviewers to be able to listen to and watch the interviewees when others are asking questions.

Table 2.3 Sample selection interview assessment record

POST   DEPARTMENT

GRADING: A= ABOVE STANDARD REQUIRED   B= STANDARD NEEDED   C= ADEQUATE
         D= BELOW STANDARD DESIRED   X= IRRELEVANT

CATEGORY	COMMENTS	GRADE
PHYSICAL CHARACTERISTICS		
EDUCATION		
EXPERIENCE		
PERSONALITY		
SPECIAL SKILLS AND CIRCUMSTANCES		

DECISION AND REASONS

SIGNED _____ DATE _____

Appraisal interviews

A normal part of any manager's work is to give feedback to his staff on their performance and behaviour. This enables adjustments to working practices to be made, problems avoided and ensures that the expectations of the manager can be met. The value of appraisal interviews is that it formalises this process.

Most managers believe that they give recognition and credit when it is due. Yet many employees will state that the only way they know that they are doing a good job is when they are not being told off. The reality is that in the pressures of day-to-day work, it is very difficult not to focus on the problems while ignoring the things that go well.

An appraisal, assessment or performance interview gives the opportunity to redress that balance. In addition, where there are problems, a formal interview gives the opportunity to consider the problem calmly and to agree solutions to it, away from immediate pressures. A problem of this sort, raised at an appraisal interview, will normally have been discussed previously. The interview situation allows both parties to examine that problem without the need to allocate blame. The discussion can centre on solutions.

Appraisal interviewing has often been unpopular. It is easy for a manager to use the situation as an opportunity to tell the interviewee off for all the things the person has done wrong since the last appraisal interview. In addition, most adults find assessment of a formal kind difficult. Nobody is perfect, there will always be cause for complaint or scope for improvement.

This is not the aim of such a system and it should not become the outcome. If blame or punishment is necessary, it should always occur at the time of the 'offence'. Appraisal interviews work best when they are aimed at improving performance and not when they are a substitute for the disciplinary procedure.

Appraisal interviews should be conducted by the person's line manager (i.e. the person to whom the employee reports). The main purposes of appraisal interviews are:

- to let the person know how well her performance is meeting expectations

- to clarify what those expectations are

- to discuss the next set of actions needed and how the manager will support the person in carrying those out.

Those not familiar with formal appraisal systems may be unused to getting direct feedback and may have no expectation of being criticised for their work. This can be at its most obvious where the job requires a high level of skill or education, such as in teaching. Often members of staff consider that their view of how the job should be done is at least as valid as that of the senior teacher. They are, therefore, more likely to resent anyone else telling them how to do their jobs.

A difference of opinion with their manager, in how the job should be done, will often be seen precisely as that, a difference of opinion. They may not always be willing to accept that the line manager is right simply because he is the manager.

The purpose of appraisal is not to change such relationships. What it will do is bring into focus those areas where the manager or senior teacher does have clear expectations about how the job should be done. Disagreements arising out of this are not caused by having an appraisal system but they may be brought out into the open by it. Arguably appraisal could reduce such problems. By defining his expectations of performance and reinforcing those at an early stage, before there is a problem, the likelihood of their developing into a serious matter is reduced.

Improvement of performance is more likely if the following is adhered to:

• Give information on how well the person has done.

• Identify problems at an early stage and identify with the problem.

• Give help and support in overcoming problems rather than trying to allocate blame.

The following is critical if this is to happen:

• Wherever possible, keep the feedback factual, what was actually done or said.

• Ask the person for her opinion on the factual feedback, particularly if it is negative.

• Discuss how performance could be made acceptable.

• Take ownership of the problem. 'You did well but we have a problem.' The same applies to failure. If something did not work as expected, the approach should be: 'What could we have done differently?', or 'What will we do differently next time?'

• Get the person to set targets for improvement.

• Most people are willing to review their behaviour or performance critically when they do not feel under threat or the need to defend themselves. Keep blame out of the discussion, therefore.

• If there are a lot of problems in the person's performance then it is probably better to focus on one or two aspects. Otherwise, the danger is that there will be a 'no win' situation. However hard she tries there will always be something wrong.

In choosing which aspects to focus on, the most serious matters, and the easiest to make headway on, are usually the first choices. The most serious, because that gives the clearest signal of improvement. The easiest, because behaviour occurs in patterns, and problems, in particular, often come in clusters. If the person can break any part of the pattern then it often opens up the possibility of tackling the other behaviours in the cluster with more hope of success. Choosing an easy target also builds confidence in the approach.

The person should be aware of the broad range of issues that need to be tackled but should be focused on a few.

There is often a standard format for appraisal interviews (see Table 2.4). The structure of the interview is dictated by the headings used. These will vary, depending on the purpose of the system. In some, the emphasis is on the review of performance. In others, planning for the future, with changes and training will be the main focus.

Job description

Give a brief overview of the duties and responsibilities of the person's job. At this interview, the job description can be amended, by agreement, to reflect changes over the last period or likely changes over the next period. In addition, the employee is given feedback, preferably factual, on his performance in each of the main areas.

Discussion on areas of difficulty tends to be the main focus, together with acknowledgement for the parts done well. Changes in the emphasis of various duties and responsibilities often form a large part of the discussion and agreement.

Teamwork

The interview should contain a discussion on aspects relating to the employee's performance as a team member, again with reference to and planning on any areas of difficulty.

Communication

How well does the employee participate in the communications within the department and with other departments? Communication is a two-way process and to be effective everyone should participate in appropriate ways. Without good communication attempts to improve standards in any school will fail.

Targets

There should be a review of the critical performance aspects of the person's job and how well these are being dealt with. Discuss any problem areas. Normally, at this stage, the issue of good performance within a school context and how it applies to that person's job is discussed.

This is, essentially, a discussion about how well the person has met previously set targets and an agreement about future performance targets (the review of performance against targets is usually done early in the interview but future targets will probably not be set until the end).

Career development

How would the employee like to see his career develop, with a realistic discussion on likely prospects? Training is often discussed under this heading.

Actions

Conclude with a summary of the actions to be carried out by the member of staff and the line manager, with review dates for those and the date of the next appraisal interview recorded.

Table 2.4 *Sample appraisal interview record*

EMPLOYEE'S NAME	DEPARTMENT
MANAGER / APPRAISER	DATE OF APPRAISAL

JOB DESCRIPTION	
DUTIES/ RESPONSIBILITIES	COMMENTS
TEAMWORK	
COMMUNICATION	
TARGETS 1 2 3 4 5 6	

CAREER DEVELOPMENT

ACTION	PERSON RESPONSIBLE	BY WHEN
1		
2		
3		
4		
5		
6		
7		

DATE OF NEXT REVIEW   SIGNED BY BOTH PARTIES

Additional points

In some organisations the employee gets a copy of the comments prior to the interview. This is generally not a good idea. If the person misinterprets a comment this can dominate the whole interview. It is better if the person making the comments has the opportunity to explain them as they are being made. However, it is good if the person knows that she is going to have an appraisal interview and has the opportunity to prepare her own thoughts on performance, personal development and the other issues.

Sometimes this type of review is used as the means to decide on pay and bonus matters. At first sight this can seem sensible. There is a link between pay and performance. But if money is brought into the balance, it tends to dominate the interview with the opportunity for review and discussion of other aspects being lost or sidelined. It is better, therefore, if money is not part of the discussion.

The frequency of appraisal interviews can vary from monthly to annual, depending on the circumstances. New staff or rapid changes in expectations make more frequent review necessary.

Many schools have introduced appraisal systems which have been designed by the local authority with somewhat different aims than those discussed in this chapter. While many of the same principles apply, the purpose of this chapter is not to encourage senior teachers to breach the requirements of their own scheme, but to provide a background understanding of the concept of appraisal.

Disciplinary interviews

Disciplinary interviews are difficult situations to handle well. The purpose of a disciplinary interview is not to punish even though that might be the outcome. The interviewer should be aiming to ascertain the facts of what occurred and to give the person thought to have committed the 'offence' the opportunity to tell his side of the story.

While the full requirements of proof, as needed by a court of law, are not necessary, certain basic 'rules' of fairness are important. These can be summarised as:

• Everyone has the right to privacy in having their 'offence' examined. The interview should not be conducted publicly.

• Everyone has the right to be accompanied. This is often the trade union representative but may be another person, usually another employee. By the same token, it is not advisable for a senior teacher to conduct such an interview without also being accompanied. This would normally be another manager, more senior than the interviewee.

• The decision should not be made in advance. However damning the evidence, the interview must be conducted with a genuinely open mind. Apart from fairness, which is the most important issue, any indication that the interviewers have made their minds up in advance will not be helpful should the case go to an industrial tribunal.

- If possible the interview should not be conducted by someone who has been involved in the initial incident. There is more likelihood of the interviewer having made decisions in advance and of bias. However, the individual's line manager would normally be the person to carry out such an interview (even when involved initially). Only in exceptional circumstances should this responsibility be handed over to someone else. In schools, department heads have not normally held such responsibility but this has started to change as the emphasis on management has increased. Now head teachers, deputy head teachers and senior teachers are all often involved, along with the board of governors. The school's (or local education authority's) own procedures should define the level of management involved.

- If the school has disciplinary policies and procedures these should be followed. Such procedures are laid down away from the heat of the immediate incident and will usually indicate what those who drew them up believe to be fair. At a more practical level, if there are procedures and they are not followed, it is difficult to demonstrate fairness to an outside body.

  If the school does not have a disciplinary procedure that lack should be addressed.

- People should not be disciplined for breaching rules which they did not know existed. If that is the case then only an informal warning would normally be issued. In general, the formal disciplinary interview should come at the end of more informal steps to stop the problem from occurring. It should not come as a surprise to the person. There are of course exceptions to this where the 'offence' is so serious that an informal warning is not adequate.

  The same requirement for advance knowledge should apply to the procedure itself. All employees should know in advance what the disciplinary procedures are. An aspect of this is consistency. While each case is individual, it is reasonable to expect that individuals who commit the same 'offence' will be treated in the same way.

- The theory of good disciplinary interviewing rests on the assumption that there is a gap between what the manager can reasonably expect and the behaviour and / or working performance of the interviewee. Following from this, a good disciplinary interview is one which helps to close that gap. The process of interviewing should be aimed at doing this, as should any action taken as a result of the interview.

  In very serious cases, where the misconduct has been proved the above will not apply, the outcome there is dismissal.

- The most important aspect, perhaps, is to treat any employee in the way that we would wish to be treated ourselves.

The structure of a disciplinary interview is quite similar to other types of interview.

Preparation

Details of the problem or incident should be investigated prior to the interview. Interviewers should be clear on which aspects need to be investigated and / or discussed during the interview. Preparation of the questions to be asked and the points which need answered is very important if the interview is to be conducted properly.

In addition, interviewers should be aware of the school's policies and procedures as they relate to this type of situation, and be aware of the outcome of any other recent similar cases. This will not determine the decision but may influence it. Interviewers should also be aware of the interviewee's rights and ensure that they are met in full.

Preparation also refers to organising the interview so the person knows when and where the interview occurs and of his rights to be accompanied. The two or more managers or senior teachers present also need to decide between them how the interview will be conducted, what each of their roles is, what questions will be asked and what areas need to be covered.

Opening

At this stage, the interviewee should be told the nature of the interview. The reasons why the interview is taking place and / or the offence which he is thought to have committed should be described. The stage which the disciplinary procedure has reached should also be outlined. Normally, the purpose of an initial interview will be investigatory, and this should be stated.

Main body

As in other interviews, this section is taken up mainly with questions and answers. The interviewee should be asked open questions and to comment on whether he actually did do what he is accused of and / or offer any explanation or extenuating circumstances. Answers should be listened to and further follow-up questions asked as needed, to clarify issues.

In some interviews, there is clear evidence that the interviewee has breached the disciplinary code. These are sometimes the most difficult interviews to remain calm during (for both interviewer and interviewee). Ensure that the interviewee gets his full say.

As stated earlier, questions should not be designed to catch the person out, but to get the full facts of what did occur. In most interviews, the purpose is to get improvement, so the questions should be genuinely aimed at exploring the incident or the problem. This will help to get a more positive outcome.

Decision and action

In many cases the decision is not reached at the time. If the interviewers are in any doubt about the circumstances or need to check an aspect, they should adjourn. They may simply wish to discuss the interview with one another or investigate issues raised during the interview. However, it is necessary, for fairness, that the interviewee is told the decision as quickly as possible.

In some cases the interview will end in an agreement about future actions and behaviour on the part of the interviewee and / or the manager. If this is the case such agreements should be recorded and a copy given to the interviewee as soon as soon as possible. The senior teacher must carry out any agreed actions, if she is to have any credibility in future.

Administrative follow-up

The interviewee must be informed in writing of:

- the outcome and any requirements on (or reviews of) his future behaviour and / or working performance

- the employee's rights to appeal, the time limits for this and who the appeal should be made to.

Managers should record details of the decisions made and the reasons for making them to ensure that the school's records are complete. This may be separate from or part of what is sent to the interviewee, as appropriate.

Disciplinary rules and procedures

Common disciplinary problems can be categorised as minor, serious and gross misconduct. The placement of various 'offences' into these categories will vary from one school to another depending on the circumstances in which the school operates. These may have been defined by the local education authority or other body already.

This type of categorisation is often used in a reactive way, i.e. when an 'offence' is committed, managers or senior teachers invoke disciplinary procedures. If it is used, however, to identify possible problem areas and to take preventative measures, that can reduce significantly the total number of problems. The list that follows is by no means exhaustive; each school will be able to add its own examples.

Minor misconduct

- Absenteeism or lateness.

- Failure to comply with the school's procedures with regard to absence.

- Careless work, quality of work below an acceptable standard.

- Minor breach of safety or hygiene rules.

- Misuse of school's property.

- Use of telephone for personal calls.

- Smoking in prohibited areas.

- Bringing alcohol onto the premises.

- Extended meal and tea breaks.

- Being away from place of work without permission.

Serious misconduct

- Neglect of or causing damage to the school's property.

- Neglect of or causing damage to the property of other employees.

- Neglect of or causing damage to the property of pupils.

- Dangerous physical horseplay.

- Consuming alcohol, drugs, or other intoxicants, during working hours.

- Waste of materials, in an excessive and / or wilful manner.

- Failure to carry out a reasonable instruction, given by a member of management or other person with delegated authority.

- Unsatisfactory treatment of the pupils, parents or visitors to the school.

- Use of unacceptable or obscene language or expressions.

- Extended period away from work without permission.

- Insubordination.

- Serious breach of safety and / or hygiene rules.

- Harassment or victimisation of another employee.

Gross misconduct
- Theft.

- Damage to the property of the school, other employees and / or the pupils caused by wilful actions, and / or gross negligence.

- Refusal to carry out a reasonable work instruction, given by a member of management or other with delegated authority, where the matter is a serious one.

- Disclosure of confidential school information or material to a third party.

- Falsification of records.

- Unauthorised use of school's equipment and / or property.

- Obscene behaviour.

- Gross breach of safety rules.

- Deliberately ignoring safety and / or hygiene rules.

- Intoxication induced by alcohol and / or drugs.

- Leaving the premises without permission.

- Serious harassment or victimisation of another employee or pupil.

The disciplinary code
The disciplinary code, like other aspects, tends to vary from one organisation to another. However, certain basic principles tend to underlie all codes, reflecting points which have been outlined earlier in the chapter. There are practical issues which need to be taken in account:

- The employee has the right to reasonable notice of the hearing and to be accompanied by another employee of his choice, if he wishes.

- The employee has the right to appeal the decision taken as a result of a disciplinary interview, preferably to someone not involved in the initial decision (preferably, because in some small schools or at very senior levels this is not always possible).

- Interviews and decisions should be quick. This must take into account the need for a proper investigation and the availability of those conducting the interview. Normally, five working days, maximum, between the misconduct and the hearing and three working days, maximum, between the hearing and the employee being informed of the decision.

- The objective of a disciplinary procedure is to improve performance, prevent a recurrence of undesirable behaviour and to do this in a way that is fair and seen to be fair. It is important to note that the majority of disciplinary problems are dealt with without recourse to formal procedures. It is only when informal procedures are ineffective, or when the misconduct is a more serious matter, that formal procedures are used.

- It is common to have the option of being able to suspend the employee between the misconduct and the interview, and between the interview and the decision. If this is done, the person should be suspended on full pay. If the person is not paid then it could be argued that the decision has been pre-judged. Be careful also, when suspending, of the implications surrounding that decision. For example, if a staff member, whom the senior teacher believes to be intoxicated, is sent home, that person should not be expected to drive.

Sanctions

The sanctions normally used in misconduct cases include:

- Verbal warnings. These are misnamed since they are recorded, in writing, and the person is given written notice of the warning, the reason for it and how long it will remain on their record (normally eighteen months, after which it will be removed if there has been no recurrence). Verbal warnings are given for minor misconduct. If the same misconduct is repeated within the prescribed period, then the matter moves on to the next stage.

- Written warnings. For a repeated minor misconduct, a first written warning is issued. This also records the offence, reasons and the duration of the warning on the person's records (normally, two years). If the offence is repeated again, or if the matter is one of serious misconduct, then a final written warning is issued. This also usually has a two year duration and, along with details of the offence and duration, makes clear that a repeat of the offence will result in dismissal.

- Dismissal. This is given where there is gross misconduct that has been established in the manner described earlier. It can also be given for a less serious offence that has been repeated and where the proper procedure of written warnings has been followed correctly. As with all steps, the employee should be informed, in writing, of the decision, the reasons for it and his rights of appeal, how that can be done and to whom it should be made.

Where there are mitigating circumstances the school may choose to apply one of the less serious sanctions but the reasons for doing so should be specified for the school's records.

The school should also clearly define who has the right to apply each level of sanction. Very often the decision to dismiss can only be taken at the most senior level and the involvement of someone with specific personnel knowledge is a requirement at all stages.

Other sanctions and / or punishments are possible, for example demotion is used in some organisations.

Additional points

In all written communication of decisions to the employee, her right to appeal and how this can be done should be outlined.

Appeals also should be made within a limited time period (usually within five days of the decision being received) and the person should be informed of this period. Employers seldom adhere rigidly to this.

Different types of misconduct are treated separately. In unusual circumstances, the school may take a number of offences of different kinds into account (usually minor misconducts) and issue a final written warning.

To reiterate some of the critical points made earlier:

- Before being subject to a disciplinary procedure, employees should be informed of the procedure and the rules and expectations of the school.

- In cases of unfair dismissal, the existence of a written procedure that employees are aware of, and adherence to that procedure in all respects, is critical to the outcome. Evidence of pre-judging or a failure to give a fair hearing are also important aspects. For example, having a prepared written warning and issuing it at the end of the interview would be taken as having pre-judged the issue.

- Being fair to the employee also means that senior teachers and others do not provoke the person. For example, if a person is publicly accused of theft, his subsequent behaviour might be unacceptable normally, but would be excused in the circumstances. In fact, discipline should always be carried out privately and with as much discretion as is possible in the circumstances.

If the school or local education authority already has procedures and systems in place, it is these that should be followed. In such circumstances this chapter should only be taken as giving general guidance. However, in a surprising number of schools there are inadequate formal procedures for dealing with such matters. If the school is introducing such they should be discussed and agreed with any trade unions or other staff representatives prior to implementation.

Grievance interviews

Many of the same principles apply to both discipline and grievance handling:

- The right to a fair hearing.

- Privacy and the right to be accompanied, if desired.

- Speed in responding to the notification of the grievance.

- The desirability, where possible, of sorting matters out without recourse to formal procedures.

- The existence of formal procedures, when the informal approach has not worked.

- The right of appeal to higher management.

- Confidence in the process and trust that the individual will not be victimised if the grievance is found to be unjustified.

- The fact of the existence of a procedure for dealing with problems that would develop into more serious issues if not addressed.

- In addition, care must be taken that a person who brings a grievance is not victimised or treated unfairly in any way.

Harassment in the work place

Changes in legislation have made the concept of harassment in the work place a more important one for the management of all organisations. There are some concerns that it is not possible to legislate for interpersonal relationships since no law can make us like another person. However, it is clear that a surprisingly large number of people believe that they have suffered harassment and victimisation in the work place. That is unacceptable. In schools this issue is probably seen in the context of playground bullying among pupils. However, it has equal applications among staff.

Any staff member who believes that she has suffered from any form of harassment should be entitled to raise the matter with management. In addition, any staff member who has made a complaint against a member of management has the right not to be victimised by management in terms of her future career and work. The following is an example of a harassment procedure. It is possible that the school or local authority already has such a procedure in place, in which case it is that one with which a senior teacher should become familiar.

Informal stage

Most principals and senior teachers would hope that any problems relating to harassment are the result of a misunderstanding or thoughtlessness and can be dealt with informally at an early stage in the development of the problem. It is clearly better if such is the case.

This is not to detract from the seriousness of such matters nor is it intended to discourage those who believe that they are being or have been harassed to raise the matter formally.

The informal stage will be most effective where the employee who is being harassed simply wants the behaviour to stop. An individual member of staff can seek to resolve matters by:

- Approaching the alleged harasser directly and making it clear that the behaviour in question is offensive and should be stopped. This can be done verbally or in writing.

- Approaching the alleged harasser with the support of a colleague.

- Approaching the alleged harasser with the support of a manager or senior teacher.

Where a staff member seeks the support of a manager, in these circumstances he should be advised that the manager's role at the informal stage can be one of support only. The staff member should also be advised that:

- A formal investigation and any consequent disciplinary action can only take place if the complaint is investigated under the formal procedure.

- All reported incidents of harassment will be monitored and, in the event of patterns emerging, management may wish to initiate its own formal investigation with consequent action being taken based on the outcome of that.

- A written record of the action taken will be made to assist with any formal proceedings which may arise at a later stage if the behaviour does not stop. Failure to maintain such a record will not invalidate proceedings at the formal procedure.

Formal procedure

If the behaviour continues or if it is not appropriate to resolve matters informally, it should be raised through a formal complaint procedures:

- The principal or other senior teacher will normally have responsibility for all proceedings at the formal stage. Individuals may raise matters directly with her or other senior teacher. Where an employee so requests, the school should endeavour to make available someone of the same gender, race, or religion, where appropriate, as the person making the complaint to hear the complaint and take part in the formal investigation.

- The manager carrying out the formal investigation should not in any way be connected with the allegations. In exceptional circumstances, it should also be possible for the investigation to be carried out by someone external to the organisation who has knowledge of the school's procedures.

- Another person would normally be designated by management, to assist throughout the procedure. He would attend all meetings and maintain a written record of all proceedings, including the investigation and any outcomes. The senior teacher in charge would check all such records for accuracy.

Investigation under the formal procedure
Time limits

Complaints should be raised as soon as possible following an act of alleged harassment so that the matter can be dealt with swiftly and decisively. The normal time limits should be defined (an example is given later, but these may need to be adjusted to suit individual circumstances). Where it is not possible to adhere to these then all parties will be informed of the revised time limits.

Making a complaint

It is preferable in all cases where a formal investigation is being requested that the complaint be made in writing to the principal or designated senior teacher. This should be acknowledged and a meeting arranged with the person making the complaint within three working days. If a complaint is made verbally then the designated senior teacher would confirm it in writing with the person making the complaint within three working days and at that stage either formally meet the staff member or arrange that meeting.

Initial meeting with person making complaint

The designated senior teacher meets the person making the complaint in order to:

- Clarify and record formally the nature of the complaint and that it is being handled under the formal procedure.

- Ensure that the person making the complaint is aware of the next stage of the procedure. At this and all other stages, the person making the complaint can be accompanied and assisted by a work colleague.

Avoiding contact between person making complaint and alleged harasser

The issue of avoiding contact between the two people involved should be considered before the alleged harasser is informed of the complaint.

Where a case of serious harassment has been alleged, then precautionary suspension of the alleged harasser should be considered. This would be done to enable the investigation to proceed. The individual who is going to be suspended would be informed of this at a meeting with the designated senior teacher and will have the right to be accompanied to or represented at that meeting by a work colleague.

Informing alleged harasser

The designated senior teacher would meet the alleged harasser and:

- outline the nature of the complaint

- confirm that it is being handled under the formal procedure

- ensure that the individual is aware of the next stages of the procedure.

Following this meeting the designated senior teacher would write to the alleged harasser, outlining the nature of the complaint and setting a date for a formal meeting which would normally be held within five working days of the complaint being received.

Formal investigation

The designated senior teacher and other person designated by management (referred to earlier) would form the investigating team. The purpose of the investigation would be to establish the facts of what occurred insofar as that is possible and to come to a judgement on those facts about what action, if any, should be taken. The investigating team will seek to resolve the matter as quickly as possible. The meetings with all involved would be held within ten working days of the date that the complaint was formally received or confirmed in writing. Should this not be practical both parties must be informed.

All those giving information must be allowed to do so privately and not in the presence of anyone involved in the alleged incident(s). All evidence provided to assist in the investigation must be treated confidentially except where statutory requirements place a duty on the employer to reveal it.

- Meeting with person making complaint. The investigating team would meet this person and consider both what he has to say and any other related matter. The right to having a work colleague accompany to assist or represent, at this or any other meeting, must be made clear to the person in advance.

- Meeting with alleged harasser. The investigating team would normally then meet with the alleged harasser and hear what she has to say about the alleged incident(s). The right to be accompanied would also apply here and be made clear in advance.

- Meeting with anyone who can assist with the investigation. Having heard from the two main parties the investigating team would then normally meet with anyone who can assist with the investigation. Each individual should be asked to outline what happened. It would normally be expected that a meeting would also take place with current or previous managers of the two people concerned to establish whether or not there was any history of conflict or problems between the two and / or with other people. The investigating team might wish to have further meetings with any of the individuals concerned or anyone else in order to clarify or gain additional information.

- Consideration of information. The designated senior teacher should consider all information given and consult with others as required. The purpose of this consideration is to decide whether or not the complaint of harassment is substantiated. The investigation should cover all aspects of the incidents reported, including where relevant, the behaviour of the person making the complaint. The mere fact of a person's race, gender, nationality, sexual orientation, marital status, disability, beliefs, values or practices should not be regarded as an excuse for harassment.

- Reporting the facts. The designated senior teacher would then prepare a written report outlining the facts and indicating her findings and decision as to whether or not a case of harassment has been substantiated. This report will be forwarded to the board of governors to take a decision on any management or disciplinary action.

- Decision on disciplinary action. The board of governors should consider the facts and decide either to initiate school's disciplinary procedure against one or more of those involved, and / or to take other appropriate management action (including, depending on circumstances, no further action or counselling or training).

Communicating the decision Having made a decision this would normally be communicated in writing to both the person who has complained of harassment and the person(s) against whom the complaint was made. Every effort should be made to have completed the procedure within fifteen working days of the complaint having been received. Where this is not possible those involved should be informed of the revised timescale.

Consideration of transfer Where a complaint is upheld the person making the complaint may wish to avoid further contact with the harasser. Assuming that the harasser remains in the employment of the school and where it is agreed that further contact between the individuals would be unacceptable, every effort should be made to facilitate this wish. Consideration would normally be given to relocating the harasser in the first instance. Where the person making the complaint is transferred that should not lead to any disadvantage to him.

Where disciplinary action has not been taken consideration may still be given, where practical, to the voluntary transfer of one of the employees concerned.

Counselling

Counselling may be offered to the person harassed and to the harasser. This would normally be provided by a trained member of staff or by an external provider.

Further meetings

The designated senior teacher responsible for the investigation, or other person designated for the purpose, should meet with the person who made the complaint of harassment on a regular basis to offer support and to ensure that no further harassment or victimisation occurs. This should happen even where the original complaint has not been upheld.

The person so designated would also normally be responsible for making the harasser aware of the school's policies on equal opportunities and harassment and the law relating to these matters.

3: Presentation skills

Introduction

The ability to present and sell ideas and pass on information clearly, in a variety of formats, is a critical group of skills which all managers need.

While teaching requires presentation to pupils on a continuous basis, it is surprising how many teachers feel that their presentational skills are inadequate when the audience is an adult one. There are a number of reasons for this. The formality of most types of presentation can make it difficult for some to display their natural communication abilities. An adult audience may know as much or more than the presenter. As with all skills, it is only through experience and practice that confidence and competence will come. An awareness of what is constituted by the skill will enable that to develop more quickly.

The basic requirements for good presentation are the same whatever the format and are very similar to good teaching skills. These will be examined first, followed in succeeding sections by the aspects specific to each type of presentation:

- oral presentations
- written presentations
- handling meetings.

Basic requirements for good presentation
Clear objectives

Be very sure exactly why the presentation is being made. What are the expectations that the presentation will achieve? Inform, persuade or get agreement for action are some of the more common objectives. Everything in the presentation will come back to this. It is important to be realistic, however, in regard to this.

Simplicity

To the receiver what the presentation is trying to say will often come as additional information on top of their current concerns and interests. A clear simple message will have more impact than a complex one, however well it is presented. If the message is of necessity complicated then thought must be given as to how this can be presented in a way that will build the understanding of those receiving it.

Involvement

Where possible try to involve the audience. This is important in all types of presentation. The more involved people are the more likely they are to understand.

Key points and repetition

A message will seldom be effective if only given once. Repeat or restate the message in a number of different ways. The use of summaries and key points can be particularly effective.

Illustration

Try to illustrate key points in whatever way possible. People generally take in information better when there is a visual element. A photograph, a diagram or a prepared slide for an overhead projector, with the key points outlined, are the most used methods.

However, do not let the message take second place to the method of presentation. Use presentation methods only when they suit the message.

A story or real example can illustrate a point very effectively. The presenter's own experience, if it is relevant, will often bring an otherwise dull point to life.

The audience

By audience, the receivers of the communication are being referred to, whether a written or oral format is being used. Although many presentations will have more than one audience, direct all formal types of communication at a specific individual or group. Without this type of focus the presentation will become bland and general. Even if information is included to suit additional individuals and / or groups there should be a primary focus.

Be aware of what the audience already knows and what it is not aware of. In addition, feelings and likely reaction to what people are going to be told will structure how it is presented.

Information is not usually neutral and the presenter can seldom tell the audience everything. Be selective in a way that suits both audience and the objectives of the presentation.

Preparation

Professional speakers know the importance of preparation in making them sound confident, credible and even spontaneous. It will also help ensure the presentation is focused on the audience and enhances the possibility of the objectives being met. In written presentation also, background research will be critical to credibility and effectiveness.

Oral presentations

Confidence is the additional critical skill which applies to this type of presentation. Confidence will come as a result of a number of factors.

Experience

It is unusual for anyone to be confident in oral presentation who has not substantial experience of doing it. The simple answer is to seek out those situations where oral presentations are needed without there being too much pressure.

Preparation

The importance of this has already been emphasised in the general points. There are particular aspects with regard to oral presentation. Preparation of the subject, its background and likely areas of question or challenge are important. Visual presentation to back up what is said is also critical.

Organisation

Once the material has been 'researched' it must then be organised in a logical manner. It is at this stage that the definition of objectives will become important. The order is important but so too are decisions about what to include and what not to include. One approach to this is to classify the material into four categories:

• Information which must be included if the objectives are to be met.

• Information which should be included but which might not be, if time runs out or the presentation takes longer than expected.

• Information which is relevant but which there will probably not be time to include.

• Information which is irrelevant to the objectives of the presentation, even though it might be associated with the topic or be found interesting.

Many experienced speakers do not consciously divide information into these categories, but they will be able to adjust the content of what they are doing to suit the audience, circumstances or time constraints. The inexperienced speaker is usually not capable of this flexibility unless she thinks it through in this or a similar way.

Own notes

These are intended to enable the speaker to keep track of what has already been said and focus on what still needs to be said. There are many suggested approaches to the lay-out of these and there is little to choose between them. Personal preference and what the person is used to are the main deciding factors.

One approach is to divide the presentation into a series of topics or subjects. Each one of these becomes like a miniature presentation. It has an opening, key point(s), a method of illustration and a link to the next topic. The introduction summarises the topic headings and the conclusion summarises the learning and action points from each topic.

The actual recording of what the speaker wants to say is also a matter of personal preference. It is usually better not to rely on memory. There is a danger of getting confused or even forgetting a critical point or section. Nor is it a good idea to write down every single word and then read it. Speakers who do this seldom express themselves naturally and, as a result, lose the audience's interest.

Furthermore, in most situations, the audience will be as capable of reading as the speaker. So reading notes begs the question as to why the speaker did not simply copy them and let the audience read them without him.

Recording a series of points (not full sentences) which act as a structure and guidance for the presentation works well for most people. These can also form the basis of the content of slides for an overhead projector or other type of slide presentation. This approach ensures that the points made verbally are reinforced and summarised visually to the audience.

Some inexperienced speakers are concerned that they will forget what they want to say and will 'freeze'. So they prefer that every word is written down. A compromise, perhaps, is that they record the actual words on one page and the summarised points against the script on the page facing that. They can then work from the points but revert back to the main text easily should they become stuck. Most speakers move from using this to using only the key points as they become more confident.

With reference to the content of ovehead slides – be brief. Full sentences should not be used. The slides are a reminder to both speaker and audience. They will lose impact if the sentences they contain are too long. As a rule of thumb, there should be no more than five words to a point and no more than five points on a single slide. There are many who would argue that even these figures are too high.

The exception to the above is direct quotes: it can be very useful, if a quote has particular relevance, to record it fully and display it to the audience.

Back-up notes for the audience are given with most presentations. These are intended to reinforce the message and remind the audience of it after they leave the presentation. Getting the balance right here can be difficult. People will forget what was said very quickly without some reinforcement.

If back-up notes are too long they will not be read; if too short they will not cover the subject adequately. After the audience leaves, the notes will be the only way of passing the message. A fine judgement needs to be made between what people need and what they will actually read, between giving the whole message and being realistic about the competing pressures for their time and attention.

It is better not to give the notes before or during the presentation unless the aim is to get the audience to do some work on them as part of the presentation. Even then, be careful about giving out too much too soon. It is usually better to give out only that part on which the work will be done.

The danger is that individuals will flick ahead and ruin the impact of the presentation. In this regard, as a further refinement, many speakers reveal one line of an overhead projector slide at a time to keep the audience focused on what they are currently saying. This does work in terms of refocusing the audience back every time a new point is made. The general rule is that if the speaker is simply going to read out what is on the slide, then he should reveal it all initially. If, however, the speaker wants to talk about each point, he should reveal them one at a time.

Preparation time

The amount of time needed to prepare a presentation is very variable depending on the following:

- length of presentation

- familiarity with the topic

- likelihood of being challenged by the audience

- amount of prior preparation.

Various rules of thumb are offered as guidance as to the amount of time needed to prepare and these would seem to indicate that:

- the minimum time needed to prepare is twice the length of the presentation

- the maximum that should be necessary is five to six times the length.

Both these figures could be challenged and would be difficult to justify. While experience and confidence will decrease the amount of preparation needed, it should never decrease to nil. Most very experienced speakers, even when they are making a presentation which they have given before, spend some time in preparation.

At the end of the preparation it is useful to read back over the objectives and reflect how each part of the presentation supports those. It can be effective to state the objectives to the audience at the start of the presentation and briefly refer back to them, when appropriate, to show how the presentation is meeting them.

Delivery

Relaxed and articulate is what is being aimed for and although preparation can help, experience is the most effective way to achieve this. In addition, the following points will be helpful:

- Many speakers start with a joke. This helps them to get acceptance from the audience quickly. However, it may not be a good idea for an inexperienced speaker. If the joke fails to get the expected response it can demolish what little confidence is there. Furthermore, judging an audience is a skill in itself. The joke which was hilarious when told socially may not go down as well in the context of a formal presentation.

- An anecdote which makes a point in an amusing way, or a real incident which typifies the situation being presented, may be a safer start. A story told by the speaker against himself is also popular with most audiences.

- Every part of the presentation and, preferably, every point within each part should have some means of illustration. Where this is not practical the effectiveness of the presentation will be diminished.

- Whether questions are taken during the presentation or at the end is a matter of choice. For an inexperienced speaker it may be easier to make the complete presentation without interruption. Indeed, the danger with taking questions during the presentation is that the opportunity to follow through on all the important points of the message is lost. On the other hand, the audience is usually better involved in the presentation and attention is better held.

- An audience will normally be attentive for the first few minutes. The human attention span is variable but, except in the very shortest presentations or those where the consequences of not listening are severe, a speaker can be sure that the audience's attention will wander unless steps are taken to stop it. Illustrations and examples are the means by which most speakers seek to draw the audience's attention back.

- The opening is very important for establishing interest. For presentations lasting more than a few minutes, a brief summary of the areas which will be covered is best, since that lays out what is coming and helps the audience structure the information. Outlining the objectives also helps the audience to think in terms of the use to be made of information being presented.

- Relating the information to the audience, either as a named individual or to the whole group, and its experience can help focus the individuals on the relevance of what is being said.

- Asking questions – both those which the speaker wants a member of the audience to answer and those which will be answered by the speaker – are other ways of drawing the audience back to the subject.

- In most presentations the speaker is not there to entertain. It is reasonable to expect some degree of interest and politeness. That should not be over-rated.

- Watch the audience. It will be possible to see signs of understanding, annoyance, agreement, disagreement, confusion, boredom, interest and a range of other emotions. The speaker can then adjust the presentation accordingly. He may, for example, bring in one of the less important points which, while not critical to the message, will entertain and bring the audience's attention back. The signs are usually not very difficult to recognise. But many speakers fail to notice them because they are so caught up in the presentation.

- Sometimes there will be mixed signals, some of the audience confused or bored and others involved and interested. There is no simple answer to what should be done in these circumstances – it goes back to what the objectives for the presentation are.

- Try to maintain eye contact with members of the audience. This should be neither occasional furtive glances nor long searching stares at one individual. Try to take in the whole audience, look at individuals or small groups, make eye contact with them, hold it for a short time and then move on to another individual or group. Most people have a side of the room they favour in terms of eye contact, similarly a side they are more likely to ignore. It is important to be aware of this and compensate for it.

- It is usually better to finish with a summary of main points for action or emphasise the key points of the message. If there is an expectation that those present will do something this should be clearly stated: what is expected, by when and if appropriate, how?

The outward signs of nerves can take many forms. Many people talk too quickly when they are nervous. Others develop a distracting mannerism. The individual is often totally unaware of this. The only way for speakers to discover what theirs are is to get direct feedback. This can be done by another person (be careful not to be defensive in any way since most people are usually unwilling to be critical). Probably the most reliable way to get feedback is to videorecord the presentation and watch it afterwards. This can, of course, add to nerves at the time. However, most people forget about the video as soon as they become involved in giving the presentation. Most teachers will have received feedback of this kind from pupils – whether requested or not.

There are a number of 'tricks' that experienced speakers use. For example:

- To emphasise a point put two others before it. There are then three points, each reinforcing the other. Most important points can be linked to two other related aspects.

- Naming a person who is disruptive in a non-threatening way. 'I know you have had some experience of this, John, and I think you found'. If John is being inattentive or disruptive, this will usually bring him back to more acceptable behaviour.

  Some speakers are even more direct and will ask the individual his opinion on whatever they are talking about or find some other way of putting the person on the spot.

A further step is to ask a direct question to the person about why he is being inattentive or disruptive. Teachers generally do not have major difficulties dealing with this type of problem. Their experience with pupils will usually help them here.

It is very difficult to handle this situation if the person disrupting is more senior than the speaker, in management terms, or is a parent or visitor to the school.

Generally speaking, good preparation, a presentation which addresses the needs or concerns of the audience and ensures that it is kept interested and involved, will handle disruptive behaviour by preventing it.

- Getting the initial attention of the audience is sometimes the most difficult part. If people are engrossed in conversation it can be difficult to get them to pay attention.

Turning on or off the lights of the room or the overhead projector, closing the door, closing the curtains are all approaches experienced speakers use to indicate to an audience that they are about to start. Changes in light levels can be particularly helpful.

Sometimes the easiest approach is to simply call for attention in a loud enough voice and keep on calling until attention is focused.

Another favoured approach is to start talking and hope that the rest of the audience will tell those talking to be quiet.

Speakers should be sure that they can be heard comfortably and should watch the audience for confirmation of this. In addition, they should be careful to speak with their head up and to remain facing the audience while speaking. Writing on a flip chart or board can cause problems here. The speaker will have to keep turning away. Again, this is a skill most teachers have long since developed in the classroom.

A speaker should try to be natural. Talk to the audience not at it or at the back of the room. A presentation is not a normal conversation. It is much more formal but the speaker is still trying to communicate. Talk to the audience in its own terms and in the type of language that will be understood.

Conversely, speakers should be careful of over-familiarity with a group they do not know well. If in doubt, it is better to be more rather than less formal in approach.

Speakers should not try to impress an audience with their own knowledge and learning. If an expression or word that is unfamiliar to the audience has to be used then time should be taken to explain it.

Handling questions

Many presentations end with a question and answer session or contain questions during the presentation. A number of points are important in handling questions:

- While the question is asked by one individual, the answer should not become a private conversation between speaker and questioner. The answer should be addressed to the whole audience. The presentation is being made to all of them. The danger, if the speaker starts a private conversation, is that other members of the audience will do the same. Interestingly, this point is very obvious in a classroom setting but does seem to need to be emphasised in the context of presenting to a group of adults.

- Among the most difficult situations is when speakers are asked a question during the presentation that relates to a point that will be covered later. To answer it at the time will disrupt the flow of the presentation. But to say that it will be dealt with later is not very satisfactory either. The person is concerned with that issue at that time and may be distracted from the rest of the presentation until the point is answered.

  Probably the best approach is for the speaker to point out that the issue will be dealt with later and therefore does not wish to spend a lot of time on it at this stage and then give a quick answer.

- Preparation for the points and issues that are likely to be raised is important. However, someone may still ask a question that the speaker does not know the answer to. How big a problem this is depends on how much of an expert the speaker is expected to be. Generally speaking it is better not to bluff. 'I will check that later and let you know' or 'I have not come across that problem before and so cannot answer it', for example, will prove to be satisfactory answers.

  If a speaker appears too often not to know the answer, however, credibility will suffer. An alternative is for a speaker to state that she has never come across that particular situation and then to cite similar cases and go on to say how those could be dealt with. For example, 'The nearest that I have come to dealing with that situation is'. That approach balances honesty with an opinion as to how the question could be answered. It is difficult to give absolute guidance in a situation like this. As with so many other aspects, it demonstrates the importance of good preparation.

- A further type of question to be careful of is where the speaker is asked to comment on a seemingly innocuous issue. Then the answer will be used to condemn the speaker or to ask the real question which is going to be very difficult to answer. Where a speaker sees this tactic coming it is probably better not to answer the initial question but to ask the person what their next question is going to be, or what is behind their question.

- One of the most difficult things for the inexperienced speaker to handle is when there is a period set aside for questions and no one asks any. The silence while waiting for someone to ask a question can seem unending. Often it is a matter of getting the 'ice broken', so it may be a good idea to prime someone to ask the first question. Another approach is to have a few questions for the audience. This will get people talking and make their asking questions easier.

The reason for wanting questions to be asked is that they ensure that the audience is involved and that the message is applied to the person's own circumstances. It is part of the presentation and comes back to the objectives. A typical presentation plan is shown in Table 3.1.

If the objective is to inform then questions will demonstrate if that has been done or if there are any areas of misunderstanding. If the objectives relate to action being taken (and it is usually only when the person starts to address the practicalities that action will be taken), questions will show whether or not this likely to happen.

It can be dangerous to assume that because teaching skills are good a senior teacher will not have any problems dealing with an oral presentation to an adult audience. The basic principles are similar but adults expect to be treated differently from children or young people. In addition, there is a difference between presentations in which the objective is to impart information or increase skills and knowledge and those where it is to convince, persuade or discuss an issue with an audience. This second type of presentation is less common in teaching.

Table 3.1 Sample presentation plan

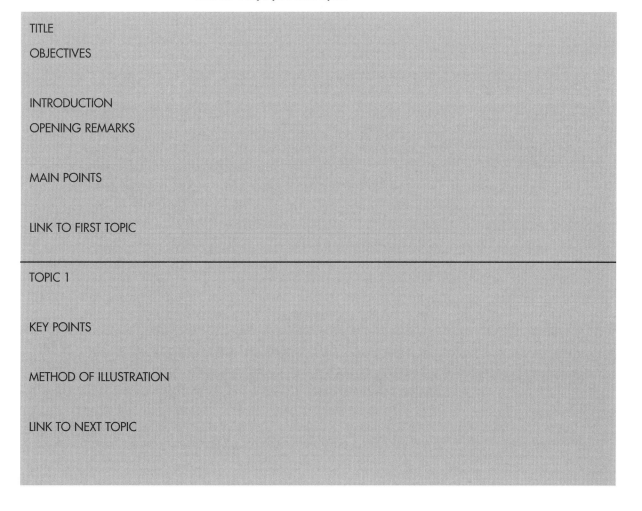

TITLE

OBJECTIVES

INTRODUCTION

OPENING REMARKS

MAIN POINTS

LINK TO FIRST TOPIC

TOPIC 1

KEY POINTS

METHOD OF ILLUSTRATION

LINK TO NEXT TOPIC

TOPIC 2

KEY POINTS

METHOD OF ILLUSTRATION

LINK TO NEXT TOPIC

TOPIC 3

KEY POINTS

METHOD OF ILLUSTRATION

LINK TO NEXT TOPIC

CONCLUSION

KEY LEARNING AND / OR ACTION POINTS

CLOSING REMARKS

NOTES / HAND-OUTS TO BE DISTRIBUTED

DECISIONS / ACTION / ARRANGEMENTS NEEDED BEFORE CLOSE OF PRESENTATION

Written presentations

Most of the same 'rules' apply to presenting written material as do to oral presentations. There is the same need to be clear about objectives and to ensure that the presentation achieves these. Expression must also be clear and logical and it must seek to involve the reader. There are some additional problems with a written presentation:

- In an oral presentation part of the meaning is put over by how the message is delivered, by gestures, tone of voice and by the way various parts are emphasised. In a written presentation it is only the words and punctuation that can do this.

- The presenter will usually have less control over the context and environment in which the presentation is received.

- The presenter will usually not be present to answer any questions. So any problems of unclear communication must be resolved before giving the written presentation to its audience. For this reason, expression needs to be more formal and less open to misinterpretation than a spoken message.

- The written word stands. What is said may be open to discussion and different types of interpretation. What is written seems more fixed. Of course, even a written quotation taken out of context can be misinterpreted but most people will believe the written word. It is less acceptable to rephrase the written word. Writing commands more authority than speaking but if a mistake or misinterpretation is made, it is more difficult to recover from.

- The biggest problem with a written presentation is ensuring that the 'audience' actually receives the message at all. During an oral presentation most people will be polite enough to give at least some time and attention. Written presentations carry no such guarantee.

- The attention span of most people is very short and unless they are engaged by written material at a very early stage there is a tendency to flick through it or not to read it at all.

Writing reports

Effective reports must be well-focused and easily accessible to the 'audience'. Reports have many different formats and purposes and it is difficult to give advice that is common to all of them. The points put forward here must be interpreted, therefore, as to their relevance and appropriateness for specific types of report. However, most of the points made are general and apply to most written documents that are called reports.

All reports should be aimed at a specific audience that has been clearly identified by the author, otherwise there are problems deciding what should and should not be included. One of the problems may be that the report will be used for a number of different purposes and with a number of different groups. If the report is to be clear and focused the author must decide precisely who the audience is and the objectives or purposes of writing that report for that audience. It might also be useful to state clearly who the intended audience is at the start of the report.

After the initial draft, the author may wish to consider the secondary uses and audiences for the report and decide how they might be accommodated without diluting the impact with the primary group.

The length of the report will determine the structure. In general it is better that the report is short rather than long. For a proposal for action, it is usually difficult to get the message across effectively if the report is longer than two (typed) sides of an A4 page. If the report needs to be longer than this then the summary should be approximately that length (or even shorter).

There should also be compelling reasons why it needs to be longer if it is a proposal for action. Project reports to external or decision-making bodies will need to be long enough to demonstrate the work that has gone into them. This sometimes applies in a working context also. A longer report demonstrates how comprehensive the investigation and analysis has been.

Length is important with regard to attention span. Most people have difficulty taking in a long or complex message and a written report should take account of this difficulty. It should be short enough to have impact and long enough to cover the points that need to be made.

Longer reports should be divided into a number of sections for ease of access. There are a number of approaches to this. For example, an investigative report may contain the headings:

- Definition

- Method of investigation

- Results

- Interpretation and discussion of results

- Recommendations and implications

- Implementation

- Outcomes

- Wider issues

- Conclusions.

An action proposal could be structured in the following way:

- Background

- Current situation

- Developments

- Proposal

- Resources, premises and equipment implications

- Recruitment and training implications

- Financial implications

- Critical success factors and measures of success

- Implementation plan

- Conclusions.

All these categories are self-explanatory: they aim to give structure and to make a long report more accessible to the reader.

All reports tend to reflect the most basic structure of:

- Introduction

- Main body

- Conclusion.

Introduction

This could also be called the summary. It gives a broad overview of what the report contains but does not go into detail. It could be compared to the summary given at the start of most news bulletins on television or radio. It tells the audience what the subject matter is going to be and acts to engage, with the hope that people will want to find out more.

Each sentence in the introduction should be the basis for a paragraph or a section in the main body of the report. The introduction is often one of the last parts of a report to be written. Alternatively, the writing of the introduction could be used to give structure to the mass of information that has been assembled and, therefore, be the first part to be written. In either event, the introduction will act to give the report the appearance of a logical structure and lead the reader towards the main body.

Main body

This is not a single section but a series of sections and / or paragraphs. It is where the main message is passed in detail to the reader and the main arguments made. The structure of the main body should reflect that.

Usually, it will open with a review of the current situation. Depending on the type of report it is, this could be headed background or current situation. Use could be made of one of the analytic techniques. For example, a SWOT analysis (i.e. an outline of the strengths, weaknesses, opportunities and threats of the current situation). Another popular analytic technique which could be used here or later in the report is the PEST or STEP analysis (this is an outline of the general factors effecting a situation under the headings of political, economic, social and techno-logical).

There are other methods and approaches but these tend to be specific to particular topics or areas of work. The analysis starts the argument as to why the action that is going to be recommended later is necessary. So the decisions that are made here about what to include or not will be critical to how well the argument is made.

The focus on the current situation can lead to consideration of the future – what is new and / or likely to develop along with possible problems and challenges. This will, of course, not be relevant to all reports.

This often leads on to a section where the problems are specified. In some reports, it is the opportunities that are defined at this stage. Again the way that this is presented or worded will be significant for the strength with which the recommendations are made later. It is here that the case for action is set out.

If any research or surveys have been carried out, these usually come next. The simplest heading for this is 'Results'. Here the key findings should be detailed. If there are additional interesting findings which would be distracting to the main thrust of the report, it is probably better to give these in an appendix. Give enough detail in the main body of the report to make the case. Anything else to be included should be put at the end for those who are interested to read it.

If findings have been formally analysed in any way, it may also be of value to give the raw data in an appendix. If the report is on a piece of research this section together with interpretation and discussion of those results will probably form most of the main body.

Reports on research should comment on the following, 'Experimental design' or 'Method' (i.e. what the author did and how the research was carried out), 'Results' (i.e. the findings), 'Interpretation' (i.e. the significance or otherwise of particular findings), 'Discussion' (i.e. the author's opinions on the significance of the findings), 'Further research needed' or 'Recommendations'.

Alternatively, if commenting on someone else's research or on a number of pieces of relevant research, the main determining factor as to how this is presented is relevance to the case the author is making.

Even if the report is a factual one into operations, it would be unusual not to present options for improvement and / or change. It is in this part of the main body that the case for that is made. For people to take action there has, usually, to be a well-defined reason to motivate them. The author is seeking to define the motivation for change. The headings of this section will again reflect what type of report it is.

Where the report is intended as description of a change which has already been implemented, the next section often outlines problems encountered and steps taken to overcome them. There is a need to be selective in what is chosen to include here. Generally speaking, if steps have been taken which would be unexpected or had not been anticipated, then it is in this section that the justification for that is offered.

Arising out of the evidence and / or information presented, the next step is to suggest what to do as a result. In a report on action already taken this section will be on the outcomes of that action. But in most reports it is proposals and / or recommendations.

These are usually better if they are written briefly. With longer recommendations there could be a brief statement, as a heading, followed by an in-depth description of what is being proposed.

If the recommendations have cost or savings implications then these can be laid out as part of this section or separately in a financial implications or financial analysis section. The most difficult aspect of this is when there are a number of possible paths to be taken and the cost will depend on decisions which the person writing the report cannot make.

The author may wish to outline the options and the cost and pay-back period of each. Alternatively, the additional costs that will be incurred and / or savings made if various options are followed could be given. Costs may not only be about the financial costs of the recommendations. They can also be about the time, effort, amount of co-operation and commitment needed to make the proposals happen.

Conclusion

The conclusion is sometimes used to outline the action that will be taken. However, in most reports this has already been done in the main body. The conclusion, therefore, becomes the means by which the author reinforces the main message, learning points or key recommendations of the report.

Like the introduction it is a summary. In the conclusion no new information or arguments should be made. Where the introduction outlines the main issues to be discussed in the report, the conclusion gives an overview of the main conclusions in the opinion of the report's author.

Format

The length of the report will determine whether the layout is in separate headed sections or simply paragraphs laid out in sequence. In either case the basic structure is still the same.

Style

The style of report writing is also important. Many of the main points have already been made when discussing presentations in general. These are some additional or restated points, as they relate to the written word.

Title

The title of a report will often be important as the means by which the reader will be enticed to read. Generally, it should be short and contain the important elements of interest. It should give the reader an insight into the content of the report. If that requires the title to be very long then it is probably better to have a short title on the most important aspect with a longer sub-title which will also appear on the cover page.

A title stated as a question appears to meet most of these criteria, however, it is usually better to avoid this type of title – it appears to be concerned with posing the question, whereas a report should be aimed at answering it.

Report lay-out

Presentation will be extremely important to the credibility that the report is given. It must 'look the part', whatever the part may be. Generally speaking, the better the presentation the more seriously the report will be taken. However, a glossy presentation with poor content will do the author no service at all. An expensive looking presentation in a context where money is short can also have the reverse effect to the desired one. Concise, neat and well-presented is what should be aimed for.

With a long report the author should give particular consideration to the reader, with page numbers, tables of contents or other means of being able to locate a particular piece of content quickly, all being important. In addition:

- Good spacing. Plenty of white space makes the text easier to read, too much white space, however, makes it look as though it lacks content.

- Wide margins. The same points apply here as in good spacing.

- Bold headings. These will make the report more accessible for the reader and will help the author to emphasise the main points visually.

- Use of indentation and bullet points. The same points apply here as in bold headings.

- Short paragraphs and sentences. These also make reading and understanding the report easier.

All these will help to emphasise and communicate key points. However, overuse of these devices or using them inappropriately will result in a loss of impact.

The writing style will vary with the type of report it is. A conversational style may not be appropriate in a scientific report. However, it is generally true that the author should try to 'speak' to the audience rather than try to impress.

Many successful professional writers believe that the secret of good writing is to get as close as possible to what they would actually say in a conversation with a member of the audience. This must be done within the constraints of the medium of writing. Generally speaking, slang or local expressions will not be appropriate unless explained. Grammar in a report would also normally be more correct than would be needed for speaking.

It is very important to stick to the point when writing. Some leeway in this is possible when speaking but not, generally, in writing.

When the first draft is completed, it should be corrected for poor expression, ambiguous comments, factual inaccuracies, grammar and spelling. Often this drafting process is about taking out repetition, simplifying and reducing the total amount written.

In addition, the author should ask whether the report achieves the objectives set for it. If not, it may not take a lot of change to make it right. It is often a simple matter of an extra sentence at the end of a section, a point restated to enhance the issue being highlighted or the removal of an irrelevant or distracting point.

Strictly speaking no word or sentence should be included which does not advance the argument, make recommendations, clarify important issues or reinforce a point already made. In reality, there will be some words which simply help the flow of expression but they should be as small in number as possible.

As with oral presentation, examples, stories, photographs and diagrams will all help to get the points across. Tables can give a lot of information in a small space.

The contents of a page and the importance of being able to compare pieces of information should also be taken into account in the lay-out.

The length of a report was discussed earlier. However, in this context a further point needs to be made. For practical purposes, the length of the report should reflect the amount of work put into it. If three months is spent preparing a report and two pages is presented, it will seem imbalanced. Equally 40 pages of a report after half a day's preparation will raise questions about the depth of what has been done.

This point, of course, raises difficulties. The person who is trying to pretend that she has put more work into the report than she actually has will make it longer. Generally speaking, extending a report artificially will be obvious to the reader. Content which is too sparse for the length is usually fairly easy to detect and, in turn, tends to have a negative effect on the reader's view of the recommendations.

Be careful of repeating words. This is almost bound to happen. Any topic tends to have a few key words, phrases and concepts. However, when a word is overused, it loses impact. In addition, a word which has more than one meaning, with all of them used within a short space, will cause confusion.

A variation on this is that a word or phrase which has a specialised meaning within a particular context may trigger the reader to react in an unintended way. Be careful about the emotional impact of what is written. Of course, it is also possible to go the other way and be so circumspect in what is said that it results in a bland and meaningless report. Some play on the emotions is necessary to hold interest and motivate to action. It is a matter of balance.

Sweeping statements are perhaps another example of this. To say that 'everyone' does something or that the reader 'must' respond in a particular way are much stronger than saying that 'some' do it or that the reader 'might wish to consider' a particular course of action. However, be aware of the likely effect of such statements. Telling a more senior manager what he 'must' do seldom goes down well and the factual inaccuracy of saying that 'everyone' does something when, in fact, most but not all do it, tends to have the reverse effect to the one intended.

Letter writing

Many of the same basic principles apply to both letter and report writing. Letter writing is presented here as a special type of report rather than as a separate topic.

Letters can be as formal or informal as the writer wishes to make them. This will be determined by:

- the familiarity of the writer with the person being written to

- their relative positions

- the subject matter

- the later use made or likely to be made of the letter.

Many of the following points are similar to those made about reports. However, a letter has a particular emphasis:

- As with any presentation, the clarity of initial objectives will largely determine the effectiveness. Why is the letter being written? Is it to thank the receiver, to inform, to complain or another reason? The person should be clear from the start what the letter is about and what it is hoped the letter will do. The receiver should also be clear at the end what, if anything, is expected from her.

- Like reports, some letters may go to more than one receiver. This should be recorded at the end of the letter. However, like reports, letters must have a clear audience otherwise they will become vague.

- With informal letters there are no rules at all. The most successful and entertaining informal letters are usually those that are written very much as the person speaks. This seems to be very difficult to do, as most people immediately adopt a much more formal tone when writing.

- Some letters are intended to set out the writer's viewpoint only, without any expectation of action. This happens sometimes when the person is simply trying to protect herself after the event. While this type of approach is not particularly helpful, there can be circumstances in which there is no other avenue open.

Handling meetings

Meetings are another special type of presentation. The set of skills which we use for normal face-to-face communication is also needed in a meeting but is different because of the numbers involved and the formality of the setting. If a group of people are to communicate in a structured and effective way, then it is necessary to hold meetings. Many teachers are sceptical of meetings because they often achieve little while giving the appearance of addressing a problem. For this reason meetings should be few in number and the time spent in meetings strictly controlled.

The arguments for having meetings could be summarised as follows:

- They enable information to be passed on quickly and problems to be sorted out with all those affected present.

- They develop teamwork and co-operation.

- They enable co-ordination of effort between individuals, groups and departments.

- Without a regular forum for views to be expressed and problems aired, individuals, groups and departments can become caught up in their own problems and lose sight of the 'bigger picture'.

- They help involve employees in developments which might affect them.

- They give members of staff information on matters which do not directly affect them but which are of interest because they affect other parts of the school.

- They can act as a safety valve, allowing matters which are irritating or annoying individuals and departments to be brought out into the open.

- Being involved in collective decision making is more motivating than being told what to do.

- They allow individual staff members to experience at first hand the objections and reservations of others to their suggestions and / or plans.

- They make individuals more aware of where their departments and jobs fit within the whole school.

Given all this, it would be expected that meetings are popular. The reverse is more common. Many see meetings not only as a waste of their own time but also as the means by which others avoid having to do work.

The reasons for so many meetings' failure to be effective could be summarised by saying that the bad working habits of individuals (and everyone has some bad working habits) are compounded by the group. The theory of teamwork is that the deficiencies of one team member can be overcome through the strengths of others. In meetings, however, the reverse seems to hold true. The deficiencies of each individual add to the final total and ensure that many meetings are ineffective.

The most commonly stated problems are:

- The meetings have no focus or direction, with people wandering off the point and nothing being decided.

- Even when decisions are made they are not acted on.

- Meetings are late starting and then have to be rushed at the end to cover the content within the time.

- Some people hold the meeting back by raising irrelevancies or spending too long discussing minor matters.

- People do not do what they agree to. This brings the whole process into disrepute, and those who do complete their assigned tasks become de-motivated.

- The same problems arise constantly and the same solutions are offered but no progress is ever made.

- There is frequent disagreement about what was decided at the previous meeting.

- Many people fail to participate fully in meetings.

- Conversely others complain that it is those who are the best talkers who do best at meetings and there can be a gap between talking about something and doing it.

- Many people fail to give any thought to the issues of the meeting until they are actually there.

- Sometimes the person chairing the meeting uses his position to foist his views onto the rest.

- If the chair fails to control the more boisterous or disruptive members then the business of the meeting is not completed.

- Some meetings, particularly those groups who meet on a regular basis, do not have sufficient content to justify the time spent.

Understanding the process of meetings

Meetings are gatherings of people structured for the purpose of communicating. Certain rules must be followed if they are to be effective. As with other management skills, these may have to be adapted to a senior teacher's particular circumstances but the basic principles hold true in most situations.

The formal parts of a meeting are in the roles and, arising from those, the procedures. There are three main roles: chair, secretary, member.

Chair (or chairperson, chairman, speaker etc.)

The person who chairs the meeting has responsibility for:

- Fixing the date, time and location of the meeting.

- Deciding the agenda and circulating it to the others attending, a reasonable period before the meeting.

- Setting the timings for the different agenda items and sticking to those.

- Giving all participants the opportunity to speak, drawing out the quieter members and stopping those who have had their say from dominating the meeting. This is a disciplinary role. It can be particularly difficult if the chair is not the line manager of those at the meeting. It can require diplomacy and strength.

- Ensuring the meeting starts and finishes on time and that the agenda is followed. However, all participating members have a responsibility to make sure the meeting is successful. The chair can only create the conditions where this might be possible.

- Ensuring that all participants get the minutes of the meeting as soon as is practical after the meeting.

- Ensuring that decisions are made, tasks are clearly allocated and a decision is made about what to do with those items where a decision is not possible.

- Reviewing decisions made at the last meeting and progress made by the members towards doing what they were charged to do. If the chair is in a line management position this may also take the form of calling to account those individuals who have not done what they had agreed. That may be done at the meeting or, if appropriate, in private afterwards.

- The chair is usually also a full participating member of the meeting but this should not be used unfairly to his own advantage. In many meetings the chair is also the line manager of those present. So it is expected that he would have strong opinions on many issues. That can make it more difficult to be fair in handling those who disagree.

Secretary (or minute taker)   In smaller meetings this role may overlap with that of the chair. It is better if this does not happen, since both roles are quite distinct and demanding.

The main role of the secretary is to record the minutes of the meeting. The minutes comprise a record of all present, the agenda and decisions taken. Some secretaries try to record discussion. This is not usually possible so it becomes a very selective record. Unless there are compelling reasons for doing otherwise, it is better to restrict the record to actual decisions made.

At the meeting the secretary has a role ensuring that it runs according to plan by alerting the chair to problems or potential problems.

Outside the meeting the secretary supports the chair in organising the meeting. For example, the secretary may be involved in drafting and distributing the agenda, arranging the location and timing of the meeting and refreshments etc. Generally speaking the chair has responsibility for seeing decisions about organising the meeting are made and the secretary has responsibility for actually doing or seeing that those decisions are implemented.

The secretary is usually also a full participating member of the meeting. This can be at odds with having to take minutes. The real influence of many secretaries comes in the writing up of minutes. It is possible to put some 'slant' or 'spin' onto the wording of a decision. Integrity is a very important quality in a secretary.

Members   These are usually the biggest number attending a meeting and it is they who have the biggest influence on whether the meeting is successful or not. Assuming that the intention of the members is to make the meeting successful the following are their main responsibilities:

- Arriving on time.

- Attending to the business of the meeting.

- Ensuring the meeting is well-run (this is the chair's role primarily but every member has some responsibility for it).

- Reading the agenda and being prepared to comment on and discuss the items.

- Not wasting the time of the other members by irrelevant comments or questions. Not wasting the time of other members by taking up the meetings time on matters which could be sorted out individually.

- Taking seriously the decisions of the meeting. Ensuring that any tasks allocated are performed, as agreed, or informing the chair of any problems in that regard, as early as possible before the next meeting.

- Being willing to state their point of view in a constructive manner. A meeting should not degenerate into a competition or a point-scoring exercise. Another aspect of this is allowing and encouraging others to have their say even those who are in disagreement. The theory of good teamwork and good meetings is that by bringing problems out into the open, better solutions are found.

- Contributing to the setting of the agenda for the meeting.

If meetings fail all the participants lose out, so it should be in everyone's interests to make them work. This may seem like an ideal, but only if everyone genuinely tries to work towards this can meetings have any realistic hope of being successful. Some additional points may prove useful:

- The contribution of all is important but not everyone will contribute equally. Some are more comfortable with that role than others and some will know more than others.

- If a senior teacher has a regular group meeting it will be inevitable that, at certain times, there will not be enough to fill the agenda properly. In these circumstances, the meeting should be cancelled. However, if cancelling becomes a regular occurrence then individuals will take those meetings that do happen less seriously. Most groups go through a cycle with meetings:

  - in the early stages of group formation they will be of value in keeping people informed of what is going on;

  - as a group of staff members becomes more familiar with one another the meeting will be of its greatest value as the place where problems can be resolved and frustrations defused;

  - the point will be reached where virtually every problem has been raised in some form or another and virtually all possible solutions tried;

  - at this stage the meeting can seem of little value. Nothing new seems to be discussed or suggested. This point is often reached about two to three years after the initial series of meetings were set up (it can, of course, happen at any time). This state of affairs will usually go on for between six and eighteen months by which time enough changes will usually have happened to make the situation sufficiently different that the meetings will be of value again;

  - unfortunately many groups give up during the difficult period and have to find a new mechanism for discussing relevant issues when the situation changes. It is important to recognise during this time what can and cannot be achieved and let the meeting temporarily change its form to accommodate that.

- Decisions at most meetings should be by consensus rather than by a vote. But, in some cases, the discussion will end in the senior teacher giving an instruction. There are few work places where everyone has an equal say. The realities of normal working life are not suspended in a meeting. What a meeting does is give an opportunity for people to have their say and influence events. It does not promise them control – no one should pretend that it does.

- Some people have difficulty making themselves heard at meetings:

  - it is important that what any group member says can add value to the discussion and that everyone demonstrates a willingness to contribute;

– catching the chair's eye is one way for a person to indicate that he wants to speak;

– alternatively, catching the eye of the person who is currently speaking can also be effective. The current speaker will address remarks to those who appear interested, setting up an expectation that they will reply or speak next;

– these subtle approaches may not work and a group member may simply have to keep repeating that he has a point of view to express until the group listens. Complaining to the chair is another possibility.

4: Managing operations

Introduction
Managing time

Before taking a management position, most people expect that they will have enough time to do the job that is expected of them. It is possibly one of the defining features of a management job that there will virtually always be more to do than the manager will have time to do it in. The wider the management responsibilities the more likely this is to be true.

If this is accepted then it follows that some parts of a senior teacher's duties and responsibilities will receive more time and attention than others. To express that in a more negative way, some parts of the job will be neglected. What is the basis for making decisions about what to give time to and what to neglect?

If left to chance, the more immediate or pressing problems will receive the attention. If the most important parts of the job are also the most immediate then that will not cause problems. However, this is rarely the case. Most time management problems arise from the confusion between what is urgent and what is important. Good time management is based on a clear understanding of priorities and the allocation of time based on that.

The work done earlier, on the purposes of the job and department, has particular relevance here. Senior teachers who have not reflected on this will be more likely to respond to the latest piece of information or the most demanding individual and will spend their days chasing one aspect or another, without ever seeming to achieve anything. Those that have given this proper consideration will be in a better position to base their responses to situations on a rational analysis of what the priorities of the job are.

Signs of poor time management

Most senior teachers display at least some of these signs at some time or another. However, poor time management is where the item characterises the whole approach to work. Senior teachers should be careful of assuming that because they identify one or more of the items as something that they have done that this automatically means there is a problem. It is the behaviours which occur continuously which need to be examined in detail.

Crisis management

This implies handling one crisis after another and never being able to rise above those crises. In particularly bad cases of this, the senior teachers come to enjoy handling crises and miss the 'buzz' when there is no crisis occurring. Everyone in a management position will experience crises from time to time but if they are a continuous feature, then behind it there almost always lies a lack of both planning and learning from past problems.

Complete the crisis management questionnaire in Table 4.1.

Table 4.1. Crisis management questionnaire

1 How often do crises occur within your area? A crisis is defined as a situation which requires you to take different or exceptional measures or which takes you away from what you should be doing. A rough estimate is sufficient.

2 What steps do you take to prevent crises from occurring? In particular, if an unexpected problem does occur, what steps do you normally take to ensure that it does not happen again?

3 What use do you make of written procedures to ensure routine tasks are performed properly?

4 In the last week what tasks or responsibilities have you had to neglect or reduce the time you would have liked to spend on them because you were handling the unexpected?

5 What are the three most likely sources of a crisis within your area of responsibility?

(i)

(ii)

(iii)

6 What simple steps could you take which would reduce the likelihood of a crisis in each of the three situations you have identified in 5?

Doing the work for other people

All managers and senior teachers should get their 'hands dirty' from time to time, where it is appropriate. This helps keep them in touch with their people and the job. However, when this happens on a continuous basis and is not part of the senior teacher's stated duties then it begs the question of why that person is a senior teacher at all. The concept of 'adding value' to the work of your staff is discussed elsewhere. If a manager spends time doing the work of subordinates then her own duties must be being neglected. This manager is also passing a message to everyone else about the importance of what she does.

As with crisis management, there are many senior teachers who actively seek this situation. Most were appointed to that position because they were good at doing the job of those they now manage. If they were good at it, they probably enjoyed it. As a result, when they are appointed senior teacher, they still enjoy doing the work. Usually not enough to do it all day every day but enough to spend more time doing it than they need.

Another aspect of this is when someone brings a problem to a senior teacher. As a manager, it is good to be able to demonstrate value or worth in the job. One of the best ways to do this is by solving a problem that no one else can. The natural reaction, therefore, is to take the problem away from the person and solve it for them. In the longer term, this is very unproductive. The next time this problem happens the senior teacher will have to do the same and the person whose responsibility the problem is will have learned nothing.

A senior teacher has a responsibility to help subordinates with their problems, but that is not the same as solving it for them. In the short term this will take more time; in the longer term it will save time.

Complete the questionnaire in Table 4.2.

Table 4.2. Doing the work of others – questionnaire

How much of your time is spent doing the work of the people who report to you? An estimate is sufficient.

If it is a significant amount of time, what are the reasons for this?

What steps could you take to reduce the amount of time?

If this is not a feature of your working day, or an insignificant one, how have you ensured that this does not happen?

Lack of planning and organisation

Most jobs have repetitive aspects. This creates the danger of trying to do things without planning, even when they are new or different. The result of this is that more time is wasted correcting the mistakes than would have been avoided had planning been undertaken.

Clearly, if the same procedure or process is carried out regularly then it does not require a great deal of planning every time it has to be done. However, much more time is lost through a lack of planning than through too much time spent planning. Most people are inclined to do first and only reflect when things go wrong.

Another aspect of the same problem relates to the time spent searching for information or indeed anything because it was not where it should be or because there was no place for it. Most people have a hoarding tendency. They like to keep close by those things which might be useful, just in case. In reality, by the time they are needed it is likely that the person has forgotten either their existence or is unable to find them in the pile of other (possibly useful) items.

Probably one of the simplest ways to ensure that at least basic planning is done is through the use of a structured planning form. Choose one task or responsibility, which involves co-ordinating the work of two or more others, and complete the planning form in Table 4.3

Table 4.3. Sample planning form

TASK	
Goals / objectives	
1	
2	
3	
Resources needed	
People involved	Their role / responsibilities

STEPS IN THE PROCESS

(BRIEF SUMMARY OF THE ACTIONS OR STEPS TO BE TAKEN, WITH DATES OF PLANNED KEY STEPS IN THE PROCESS)

DATE

1 _____

2 _____

3 _____

4 _____

5 _____

6 _____

7 _____

8 _____

9 _____

10 _____

Interruptions

Many senior teachers complain of these as being one of the reasons why they cannot get on with their work. There is some justification for this. Senior teachers have responsibility to give time to people who work for them. However, if they allow unrestricted access then they will be continually interrupted and will never have time for their own problems.

Indeed, some senior teachers find after a period of working like this that they cannot concentrate for long periods. If they are not interrupted, they will actually seek distractions, or interrupt themselves, to do something different.

As with most aspects of management there is no perfect answer but a number of approaches can help:

• Set aside fixed times to deal with routine or non-urgent problems.

• Set aside times and / or go to a place where there will not be interruptions except in a genuine emergency.

• Keep a brief note of the interruptions: record who, when and briefly why. Keep this for two weeks. Virtually always patterns start to emerge. If it is the same individual continually interrupting then having a fixed time with this individual might help. If it is the same problem from different people, then it could indicate a training need. If it is particular times when interruptions are most likely, then the problem could be to do with location and / or the tasks being done at those times.

Complete the interruption record sheet in Table 4.4 for at least one week. You may have to copy it a number of times. Following that, analyse your interruptions and, where possible, decide on a course of action to reduce the number and type of interruption.

Table 4.4 Typical interruption record sheet

BRIEFLY RECORD ANY EVENT OR SITUATION WHICH TAKES YOU AWAY FROM WHAT YOU HAD PLANNED TO BE DOING

DATE AND TIME	PERSON	REASON

INTERRUPTION ANALYSIS

PATTERNS OF INTERRUPTION

PEOPLE

PROBLEMS

TIMES

OTHER FACTORS

CONCLUSIONS

ACTION NEEDED

Making change effective

Most people will spend more time reflecting on the reasons for failure than they do on their successes. There is a great deal to be learned from failure. However, we should also learn from success. If we do not reflect on it, we tend to devalue those things that contributed towards the success. This is particularly important in the management of change.

Identify an area where you would like to make a change at work and where you realistically could change what is currently happening (you may choose an area where you are making or are about to make a change). It does not have to be a major matter but should involve other people and cannot be implemented without some resistance or questioning. Outline your actions (or possible actions) in Table 4.5.

Table 4.5. Sample actions for change sheet

BRIEF DESCRIPTION OF THE CURRENT SITUATION AND THE REASONS FOR WANTING CHANGE

DEFINE YOUR OBJECTIVES (IN MEASURABLE TERMS AND WITHIN A TIME LIMIT)

HOW WILL YOU INFORM AND INVOLVE OTHERS?

WHAT DIFFICULTIES FROM OTHER STAFF DO YOU ANTICIPATE?

WHAT ARE THE RESOURCE OR COST IMPLICATIONS OF THE CHANGE?

WHAT ARE THE BENEFITS OF THE CHANGE TO THE SCHOOL, TO THE INDIVIDUALS AFFECTED, TO YOU?

HOW WILL YOU CONVINCE THE OTHERS OF THE NEED FOR OR BENEFITS FROM MAKING THE CHANGE? (YOU MAY HAVE DIFFERENT 'SELLING POINTS' FOR DIFFERENT GROUPS OR INDIVIDUALS)

HOW WILL YOU MAINTAIN YOUR OWN MOTIVATION IN THE FACE OF RESISTANCE?

WHAT ARE THE CRITICAL SUCCESS FACTORS? (i.e. WHAT ASPECTS ARE CRUCIAL TO THE SUCCESS OF YOUR PLANNED CHANGE)

WHO ARE THE KEY PEOPLE WHOSE INFLUENCE WILL EITHER MAKE OR BREAK THE PROJECT?

Motivating staff

The question of motivation in a working context is an interesting one. While the precise motivators vary from one person to another, there are recognisable patterns in the motivation of all of us.

Money

When asked 'What motivates you at work?' most people give money as the first answer. Some insist that it is the only answer. Money is clearly a motivator but it is not a straightforward one. How hard a person works does not depend on money alone, the other motivators often have an even greater effect. However, it is true to say that without the money most people would not go to work in the first place. Perhaps the real motivation comes when we feel that our efforts are properly rewarded.

Work itself

This is a complicated factor and tends to show itself in a number of different ways: people who have pride in their work; feeling that they do a worthwhile job or supply a worthwhile product or service; work requiring skill, knowledge or ability that most people do not have; enjoying what they do; being needed or relied on. All these are examples of how the job itself can motivate.

Control

This can range from complete freedom for people to make their own decisions to involvement in decision making, to being kept informed of what is happening. Generally speaking, the greater the feeling of personal control the higher the motivation.

Others' reactions

This factor also can take many forms. For example, fear of punishment, or at a less extreme level, an unwillingness to let someone down can motivate. On another level when people's work and efforts are recognised, particularly publicly, that can be highly motivating. In its most common form, however, this type of motivation is more subtle. People's motivation is effected if: their opinion is sought or fails to be sought whether they are included with one group as a result of the acknowledgement of effort given by pay and / or other reward. All these can send very subtle signals both to those involved and to others.

Relationships

All working relationships have an effect on morale and motivation. In general, the better these relationships the higher the motivation. Very good relationships can, however, have the effect of turning what should be work into a social club. Some relationships, however, tend to be more important than others. This is usually related to the amount of contact. In addition, the strength of feeling involved is also important. These aspects are more important than whether the other person is a colleague, a manager or a subordinate.

Costs and commitment versus benefits and challenge

This is a difficult factor to measure and tends to be governed by personal feelings. The amount of effort may be weighed against the expected return for that effort. The notions of challenge and commitment will also have an effect on this balance. Understanding the complicated relationships between these four factors is what makes individual motivation so difficult to interpret.

Experience

Previous experience will tend to determine whether people approach a situation as a basically positive or negative one. These feelings may not appear logical to an outsider but will colour every aspect of the view of those involved.

Problem handling

When a problem occurs many managers may think only in terms of prevention and, where appropriate, punishment. While this cannot be ignored, the more serious issue is often why the problem occured. Where employees' actions indicate that they feel little loyalty to the school or the senior staff of the school, and little pride in what the school provides, then a more fundamental approach is needed.

It is essential to change this attitude if the school's management team's wish is to get staff to regulate their own behaviour. There is a range of reasons why individuals might behave like this :

- A tendency for the school to look for scapegoats when there is a problem.

- Decisions made without consultation or thought for the problems they could cause employees.

- No clear understanding among staff of the knock-on effects of their actions on other staff, pupils or parents.

- Lack of training or understanding of the role of individuals and departments within the school.

The problem becomes more difficult when previous decisions by management were not popular. It is often argued in these cases that the problem is one of communication. However good a manager's or school's communication is there will sometimes be a need to take hard and unpopular decisions. The senior teachers responsible are never going to be liked for that even where it is understood that they had no choice.

The important aspect, then, is to try to build a better relationship with the staff. But management must also remain consistent. If you appear to back down because 'you need them', you will lose respect. If the changes made were right and fair most people will recognise that eventually. The next moves should now be to try to involve and consult more and to give people opportunity and autonomy, insofar as that is possible.

Major disciplinary problems often present an immediate issue of handling but there are usually more serious background causes which also need to be addressed. It may, of course, simply be part of a development process. At various stages of our employment problems could be anticipated.

Often the problem is that the school is seen as only interested in its own aims, at any cost to the employees. Sometimes the employees may feel that they are not respected or valued, by senior teachers in particular. The more managers understand why staff members are acting the way they do, the more likely they are to be able to solve the problem.

Clear goals and targets will be important. Opportunities for learning and advancement will help. Staff opinions should be sought, and listened to, when changes are being planned as this will also improve motivation. Most important of all is recognition for what was done well within a context of recognition for achievement throughout the school.

Perhaps one of the most worrying situations for any manager is when the good employee 'goes off the boil'. Managers are often divided in how best to approach this type of situation. Some feel the person needs a sharp reminder and take, essentially, a punitive approach. The basis of this is that the employee has become complacent and needs reminded of the realities of working life.

Others take a more caring approach. If this employee is now demotivated there must be reasons for it. Therefore, they identify those, let the person know of their concerns and fears if things do not improve and offer help and support. Both approaches have some merit. The second is more likely to develop loyalty in the long term. The first approach will achieve its results more quickly.

Teamwork

In motivational terms it is often in working with others that the most satisfaction comes. The characteristics of an effective team are similar, whatever the context in which that team operates. Some of the best examples of teamwork can be seen on the sports field. The difference between a good and a bad team performance is easily recognised. The biggest difference between a group of individuals and a team is that the team's performance is better than the performance of the individual team members when added together.

There are some accepted characteristics of effective working groups.

Interpersonal relationships

They do not have to like one another, although that can help. The working relationship must be good and there must be mutual respect for one another's abilities.

Clear understanding

Not everyone can be the leader, effective teams have leaders but they also have those who will do the boring and routine tasks.

Clear goals

Without this people will pull in different directions.

Openness and honesty

Disagreements are out in the open. In an effective team everyone will know where everyone else stands on virtually any issue. There will be a clear means of keeping one another informed and of airing difficulties. The effective team will have more open arguments. The ineffective team is one in which people are afraid to raise controversial issues.

Trust

Trust must extend in every direction. Once team members lose this trust in one another, then they become a series of individuals again.

Success

While it is possible to be unsuccessful and still have a good team performance, in reality it is difficult to maintain a team performance without success.

Atmosphere

There is a 'buzz', or a hum of activity, about an effective team that is lacking in the ineffective one.

Reaction to change

Generally, effective teams are constantly seeking to improve and looking for new ideas. The effective team will welcome outside views. They may be very critical of them but will seek out different approaches. By comparison, ineffective teams will be suspicious of outside help and tend towards being inward looking.

Awareness

Effective teams are aware of themselves as teams and tend to reflect, from time to time, on how good their teamwork is.

The characteristics of ineffective teamwork, by the same token, tend to be the reverse of those already mentioned, with some additional aspects:

- A lack of development of team members arising out of the resistance to change.

- Petty complaints and grievances. The focus on themselves and on maintaining the status quo usually results in a negative approach to everything.

- A lack of communication at all levels. An ineffective team will often have no obvious arguments among its members. Often they will simply not meet and discuss matters because it will be pointless, for the reasons mentioned earlier. The differences of opinion will be hidden, therefore.

- Working in isolation. Much good work is often done by individuals in ineffective teams. The problem is that much of the benefit is lost because the person is working without help or support and the work of others may inadvertently be contradicting the efforts of the individual or at least not making best use of their combined efforts.

Leadership

The difference between good and bad leaders has been the subject of speculation for many years. Both military and political leaders have been a particular object of study because of the 'publicness' of their leadership. One difficulty has been separating our feelings for the people, and the type of decisions they make, from their ability as leaders.

Research into leadership has often tried to identify the characteristics of successful and unsuccessful leaders. This has not been particularly fruitful. It would seem that there are no absolutely essential characteristics that will work in every situation. However, clearly certain approaches are more successful in some situations than other approaches. The successful leader is often the one who can read the situation and match his approach to that.

Successful leaders do seem to have certain aspects in common:

- A clear goal (sometimes called vision) of what they want to achieve.

- A definite plan as to how they hope to achieve that vision. This is usually made up of a series of sub-goals or steps towards achieving the main goal.

- Strong communication skills, at least where their vision is concerned. It would seem that the main aspect of this is the ability to get the message across to others. A secondary aspect is the ability genuinely to listen to others.

- Strong personal commitment to the plan.

- The flexibility to be able to change the plan, as circumstances change, and still keep the final goal in view.

The process by which effective leaders motivate others to achieve those goals can be variable. This aspect could be referred to as the 'approach' to leadership. There is no absolute right or wrong leadership approach. However, some approaches suit certain circumstances better than others. These are defined in many different ways.

'Tell them what to do and how to do It' approach

This is also referred to as an autocratic or directive style. It is effective when the group being led is new or inexperienced. It is often the most appropriate approach in a crisis. However, when these two aspects are not present then the approach can be counter-productive. Most people work harder if they can have some say or decision-making responsibility and if they can feel ownership. Telling someone what to do and how to do it, when they are capable of contributing more, will seldom get the best from people.

It is also true, however, that many people are happy to work for what is called a 'benign autocrat'. That is a leader who expects full obedience but in return will look after her people.

'Rules and procedures' approach

This is sometimes called a 'bureaucratic style', in another context it could be called a 'coaching' approach. All schools, except perhaps the smallest, have a need for rules and procedures. They ensure fairness and make clear where decision-making responsibility begins and ends.

This approach is often the first step away from a directive style. People are given some leeway to make decisions within tight guidelines. Where there is a need for clear accountability and where the ability to trace precisely, who did what and when, is important, then this approach is useful. For this reason the public sector tends to favour it. Its drawbacks are that it can become more important to follow the procedure than do the right thing. The approach also encourages people to 'cover their backs' rather than do their jobs properly.

Some elements of it are important in all schools, but it can be frustrating to work in an environment that has this as the main approach to leadership. In addition, it can stifle imagination and vision. But it does allow people to develop within a well-regulated structure and for most employees, at the stage of trying to develop skills and confidence, this is an appropriate way of giving them the help and support they need.

'Consult and involve' approach

Probably the most popular approach, insofar as when asked, most people would like to lead or manage like this. Conversely, it is fairly rare to find a senior teacher whose people are quite as sure that this is the way they are managed. This type of leader is sometimes called 'democratic', in the sense that everyone is given a say and has an input into the decision-making process. It has also been called a 'supportive style'.

With capable and highly motivated employees this approach has clear advantages. The employees know what they are doing and how to do it. With the help of the leader they can develop themselves and the job to a degree that is often surprising.

The approach, however, does not seem to suit the following situation:

- crisis

- where the employees are inexperienced

- where individuals lack motivation for the task.

This style is based very much on trust. Giving trust and then taking it away when it is abused by a few is very difficult to do.

It can also appear to be a weak style of leadership. Some people assume that because they are being asked their views this means that the senior teacher does not know what to do. In particular, those who are used to being directed find it hard to respect this type of leader.

However, in terms of creativity and productiveness this or the next approach will get the best results when used in the right circumstances.

'Stand back and let them get on with it' approach

This is also called a 'laissez-faire' or delegatory style of leadership. With very capable, well-qualified, confident and highly motivated employees who know what is expected, this approach comes into its own. It is probably most used as a way of managing professional staff or highly qualified groups of employees. In these circumstances, the employees may know as much, or even more, than their manager. The traditional role of the manager in giving advice and guidance is inappropriate. The employees are, therefore, given day-to-day control over their own work and decision making.

It is in this respect that it varies from the 'consult and involve' style. There, the manager gets input and opinions but will still take decisions. In this case, the person is left to make her own decisions, within very broad parameters. As with the previous approach, it uses the natural motivation and pride in work of the individual to get the best from her.

However, should problems arise, if the trust is abused or if the person takes on a task beyond her ability, there will be major problems.

First, the problems will not be easily identified. The senior teacher is standing back, so he is very unlikely to anticipate problems and even when they occur is unlikely to realise what is happening until too late. The employee is also unlikely to draw a problem to the senior teacher's attention, until matters are very serious. She will usually value her freedom and autonomy too much to want to involve anyone else.

Second, it is difficult for a senior teacher to take action on such a problem without taking responsibility away from the employee. Often the strongest reaction comes from other employees who will then believe that their own position is being unfairly undermined. In these circumstances, one person abusing trust does have a detrimental and unfair effect on others. The approach works best with a mature, capable, experienced, motivated and trustworthy group of employees.

Because of the risks it is probably the least used approach to leadership. In theory, however, it is what all managers should be aiming for with all staff members.

The approaches overlap one another. In most schools it should be possible to identify examples of all of them. However, it is usually the case that one dominates the approach to the management of a school and most of us as leaders or senior teachers are more comfortable with one approach than the others. As is clear from these descriptions, all the approaches have their place and are more appropriate in some situations than they are in others. Even with the same employee, it is possible that the style of management would change from being very directive to standing back and letting her get on with the job over a period of some years.

There is a range of deciding factors involved in which approach to use.

The task/job

All jobs tend to fit one approach better than others. For example, where a large number of people are working together and the performance of each one depends very closely on the performance of the others then a 'tell them what to do and how to do it' or a 'consult and involve' approach usually works best. However, where the task or job involves a number of people doing the same thing, and consistency is important, then 'rules and procedures' will be important. If, however, the task is one which depends on the skill and ability of the individual then the 'stand back' approach might work best.

The people

Two factors are important here. The experience, skill and knowledge of the individual employees and their commitment and motivation. As these rise, then the most suitable approach changes from 'tell them', to give them 'rules and procedures', to 'consult and involve' them, to 'stand back and let them get on with it'.

Unfortunately, these two factors tend to operate separately. For example, people, upon first taking on a new job, are usually more highly motivated than those who have done the job for a long time. The 'stand back' approach only works if both factors are present. The 'tell them' approach is probably the only way sensibly to treat new employees. The choice between 'rules and procedures' and 'consult and involve' is usually based on experience. The more knowledgeable the person the more he can contribute.

The school

Certain styles and approaches work better in some schools than in others. All departments will be affected, to some degree, by the way the school is managed. This approach usually comes from the top. While it is possible to have a different approach than the dominant one in the school it will still influence the department head's management approach.

Another aspect of this relates to personal preference. Some approaches sit more easily with one individual manager than with others. It is probably true to say that very few people would be comfortable with every approach. Equally, most senior teachers would be able to switch as different situations and individuals required.

The choice of approach should be based on an assessment of all three factors. Often, however, the senior teacher is chosen initially because her approach suits the circumstances, people and school. In a changing situation there will be difficulties if flexibility does not exist within the school to change the leadership approach to suit changing needs.

Leadership case studies

It would be useful to think through some of the implications of the different styles in different situations. A series of six case studies follows. Read each and consider how the different styles of leadership would be applied. There is no right answer in each case and the actual style chosen should suit the particular circumstances of the school. However, it will become clear that some answers are definitely wrong in some of the case studies and some of the options would be more effective than others.

In each case study assume that you have the authority and responsibility to take action.

CASE STUDY 4.1

You are at the start of a new development. There is history of change being badly received by the staff in your school / department. The planned change will involve new ways of working and will require all staff to be trained in these new ways. This will not be popular.

Tell them approach

Rules and procedures approach

Consult and involve approach

Stand back approach

CASE STUDY 4.2

The school or department in which you are a senior teacher has only recently been formed. The new staff are all reasonably capable of doing their own jobs but do not yet work together as a team. This is starting to cause problems, with some work being done twice and other aspects being seen as no one's responsibility. You are starting to get complaints about this.

Tell them approach

Rules and procedures approach

Consult and involve approach

Stand back approach

CASE STUDY 4.3

The staff in your school or department have been working together for a number of years. In the past, it was generally regarded as being successful but, more recently, there have been a number of problems. It would seem that, because of the past success, most staff have become complacent. They believe that they do an excellent job when, in fact, it is little better than acceptable. In addition, a number of 'unhealthy' working practices have crept in.

Tell them approach

Rules and procedures approach

Consult and involve approach

Stand back approach

CASE STUDY 4.4

You have been given responsibility for a project that has run into difficulties. There are many theories as to why the previous person in charge could not get it to work but there is no doubt that the current group has lost confidence, both in itself and in the project. You believe that it can work but everyone needs to focus on an own role in the project and need to be more realistic about what is achievable.

Tell them approach

Rules and procedures approach

Consult and involve approach

Stand back approach

CASE STUDY 4.5

There are no serious problems in your school/ department. The performance of all the staff is reasonably good and there are no major interpersonal problems. You feel, however, that they could perform much better. You are concerned about creating problems, where none exists, but if you do not take action there is a danger of complacency.

Tell them approach

Rules and procedures approach

Consult and involve approach

Stand back approach

CASE STUDY 4.6

You always believed that your relationship with your staff was good. However, this morning a more senior person (the school principal or school inspector) has brought a letter of complaint about you, which he has just received. The letter is anonymous but refers to events that only a member of the school or department would know about. The person complains that you are high-handed, never listen, treat them like children and try to rule by fear. The letter also states that this is the view of the majority but that everyone is afraid of your reaction and so would not speak out. The senior person leaves the matter with you to deal with initially, but wants you to report back to him what you have done.

Tell them approach

Rules and procedures approach

Consult and involve approach

Stand back approach

5: Financial management

Introduction

This chapter focuses on financial issues. Schools have been given increasing control of their budgets and this process is likely to continue. Systems and procedures for managing finances are either already in existence in most schools or will be dictated to the school by an external body. Rather than focusing on those procedures therefore, this chapter is aimed at broadening the understanding of senior teachers who traditionally have not had to think in financial terms.

Reward and bonus systems

These are most commonly used in sales and production environments. However, they can be effective in all settings and approaches such as performance-related pay have become an increasing feature in many different sectors, including schools.

These systems usually seek to motivate staff by defining the outcome for good performance in monetary terms. It has been argued that this approach has wider applications than those that relate only to money. Any reward for good performance or achievement should be included. This requires the senior teacher and school to be constantly looking for the positives and to be focused on the opportunities to reward good performance rather than to punish bad performance or behaviour.

At first sight, many senior teachers do not think that they have many motivators at their disposal in relation to the staff. Indeed, it is often a feature in the early stages of this approach that tangible rewards such as money are used. A senior teacher does have control over the working environment of staff members and after the initial uncertainty, opportunities for reward and recognition become more obvious.

The characteristics of an effective system of reward are as follows:

- Everyone is clear on exactly what constitutes the rewarded behaviour and what the reward will be.

- Reward follows automatically on the standard being reached.

- In larger organisations, there is a common system in operation.

- If an employe who 'qualifies' for a bonus or other reward finds that performance falls in another way, the reward is still given. The employee may also be 'punished' in another way.

- Rewards should be something extra and not simply something that the employees regard as their right anyway. That will be perceived by the employees as a removal of something desirable for poor performance rather than a reward for good.

- The most effective rewards tend to be those which allow the staff member autonomy in his work without intervention from above. Material rewards in themselves seldom motivate for long. The effectiveness of any system tends to be related to the ease with which employees understand it and their confidence that the rewards earned will be honoured.

- Reward and bonus systems should be aimed at enhancing performance. In virtually every working situation this means teamwork. Individual bonus systems tend to work against this. A bonus or reward system should be focused on the team rather than the individual, but must recognise and reward genuine effort.

- There is a danger of rewards or bonuses becoming the norm, in which case they lose their ability to motivate. Worse still, if they become expected, then not receiving one becomes a punishment.

Costs and finance

This section is not intended as an introduction to accountancy. All senior teachers need some understanding of how finances are managed and costs tracked. The purpose of this section is to explore some of the ways in which costs can be calculated in order that better control can be maintained over this aspect, and to introduce some basic financial concepts.

Throughout this book there has been an attempt to keep jargon to a minimum. All topics have their own language and whatever steps are taken, it is inevitable that some of that jargon will creep in. In finance, the jargon is the starting point for understanding the concepts. Many financial concepts were developed in a business setting. They have been applied to schools here.

Before outlining some of the basic concepts it is important to note that good financial management is a reasonably straightforward matter. First, there are outgoings, which are what is paid for, the objects and services that are bought. These include the cost of labour (wages, among other things), accommodation, heat, light, materials, resources and equipment.

Second, there is income, the money received for the goods and services supplied. In a work place, where money actually comes in, this is fairly easy to identify. However, in many places it is not so easy to calculate. A department in a large school will have difficulty calculating its income when it makes a contribution towards the products and services of the school but does not actually produce products or deliver services that are paid for directly. Some of the accountancy practice in schools is aimed at helping senior management keep track of the outgoings and income of such departments.

Basic financial concepts

This is by no means an exhaustive list. The choice of items is based on those which senior teachers should find useful and relevant in most management situations.

Costs

These are part of the outgoings of the school. They can be categorised in many ways. For example, in industrial settings, it is common to classify costs as:

- those relating to people

- those relating to capital items such as, equipment or machinery

- those relating to materials or expendable items, i.e. things which are purchased, used and then need to be repurchased

- those relating to other parts of the operation not easily :
  the previous three (for example, advertising costs).

One of the aims of finance departments is to be able to allocate
that they can be monitored and controlled. The fear of many managers .
are allocated costs over which they have no control. As a result, they might be no
accountable for costs about which they can do nothing.

Costs refer to all monies that the school has to pay out. Sometimes the concept of
'prime costs' is used. These are costs that relate solely to labour, materials and
overheads which are directly involved in producing the product or providing the
service. Prime costs in a school would be those directly associated with delivering
an education service. School meals would be an example of something excluded
from prime costs.

Cost and profit centres

It is in relation to the allocation of costs that cost centres come into play. They are
areas within the organisation where costs can be allocated. The purpose of this, as
already stated, is so that costs can be monitored and controlled. In a large school if
this, or a similar means of identifying where the money is going, is not in place,
then the danger is that spending will spiral out of control. It is an unfortunate
aspect of human nature that if we believe that no one cares then many people will
spend, or use materials without thought of value for money or what their genuine
needs are.

Cost centres are usually based on the lines of the normal departmental structure
in any organisation. This means that individual managers or senior teachers can
control and be held accountable for their own costs. So while a senior teacher or
the bursar /finance officer may do all the actual buying, for accounting purposes
the cost of those purchases will usually be allocated to the department for which
they are purchased.

While this sounds straightforward it can often lead to difficulties. For example,
when two departments use the same books or learning materials and the amount
of use each makes is different, attributing costs can be difficult. Even more
difficult is allocating a cost one department incurs doing work for another, for
example the caretaker ordering equipment to be used within only one or two
rooms or departments.

In theory, only certain activities generate any income, so all costs must be
allocated to them eventually. In this model, the administration or caretaking
department, for example would charge all the other departments for the service
they provide. This, of course, is only a 'paper' exercise but it is often the means by
which senior teachers can judge the performance of the support services which a
school has. The scope for disagreement within this is immense.

For example, if there are five education departments in a school and an administration department, management will want to allocate the cost of running administration to the education departments. On what basis should that be done?

- It could divide the costs by five but if the departments differ in size and the amount of work done for them by administration that would be unfair.

- The numbers of pupils taught by the department could be another basis, so that the departments with the bigger teaching commitments took responsibility for a bigger amount of costs. At first sight that may seem fairer, but there may be no relationship between numbers of pupils taught and the support given by administration.

- Cost allocated on the amount of support given would seem fairer but could be very difficult to calculate.

- Numbers of staff could be another basis, as could square footage of the classrooms used by the department but both these would be no fairer than any of the others.

- The picture could be further complicated if some of the administration were provided by people who also had teaching responsibilities in one or more of the departments.

There is often no simple answer. An understanding of the basis on which costs are allocated and an awareness of the problems that this might cause are the most important elements for senior teachers.

Within this approach, the concept of profit centre is sometimes introduced. Stated simply, a profit centre is a number of cost centres lumped together in order that they show income as well as outgoings. In this context, the performance of the profit centre can be judged on the comparison of outgoings and income, in terms of profit and loss. This may seem to have a little relevance in schools. However, as finance moves towards formula funding and support for special projects, the case for thinking of school departments as profit centres becomes more feasible.

Absorption costing

This is a method of costing which seeks to allocate all costs to a cost or profit centre. In the final analysis, all schools must face the 'bottom line', when they subtract all outgoings from income, what are they left with. However, managers often complain that absorption costing can allocate costs to them that they do not spend themselves and therefore cannot control. So while being able to account for every expenditure is important, a senior teacher may not be able to do anything about some of the costs that her department has incurred.

From an organisational viewpoint, any cost which cannot be classified and attributed to a source will usually be abused. The problems of absorption costing should not detract from its benefits, therefore. The debate on who spends what, and how justifiable particular expenditures are, is important to the financial health of all schools. Poorly controlled expenditure robs a school of the benefits of its other activities and of its income.

In costing it is important to differentiate those situations where there is no additional cost to the school. For example, if three teachers meet for the day what does that cost? If they meet in the school's own premises, using a room that would have been heated and lit in any event, assuming that their teaching commitment could be covered from within existing teaching resources, then there is no additional cost to the school. The costs of their salaries for the day would have been paid whether they met or not. All these items are a cost to the school. They are not additional costs, however.

Practical exercise in costing

It would be useful to carry out a costing exercise to experience these problems at first hand. Using your own school and department select one of the activities and cost it. Where possible use real costs; however, if this is not possible, estimate using your knowledge and the best guess you can make of the various costs. Include the cost of labour (this can be averaged if there are different rates) materials, heat, light and any other relevant expenditure.

Give the basis for your estimates. For example, the cost of lighting could be based on your estimate of the number of lights used for the length of time the operation took place, based on the information that the electricity companies supply about the costs of a unit of electricity. The estimate for heating costs could be based on the total cost of heating the building for a quarter divided by the percentage of the building your department uses and the percentage of a quarter that the operation took. While the exercise may not have immediate applications, it will contribute to your understanding of costs and will enable you to cost a new activity should you have to present an estimate at some later time. It will also help you understand how difficult such costings are and the assumptions that are needed to carry out this exercise.

The balance sheet

Modern accounting is based largely on the notion of what is called 'double entry' bookkeeping. This comes from the concept that every entry on the books has a positive and a negative aspect to it. If computer equipment is bought, for example, that is a loss of the money you used to buy it. It is also a gain, in that the school now has something of value – and that value could be because of its use in the school or its resale price.

The terms debits (money coming in) and credits (money going out) are used. These terms are probably the most confusing to people who are not accountants because most believe that credits and debits are the reverse of this. Perhaps the fact that bank statements are expressed in this way is the reason for the confusion. In fact, the bank statement is a statement of the customer's account from the bank's (and not the customer's) point of view.

The balance sheet seeks to lay out these entries in a manner by which a manager can see how well or badly the school is doing financially. With the double entry notion the two sides of a balance sheet should 'balance'. A balance sheet, however, only gives a snapshot of how the school is doing. It can be misleading in that respect, but is a source of factual information on financial performance at any one moment in time.

The balance sheet's two sides are made up of assets and liabilities.

Assets

Assets include money, machinery, equipment, buildings, land, stock, and debtors. In some balance sheets, goodwill could also be shown as an asset. Assets can be difficult to value. For example, the computer equipment mentioned earlier, even if it was left in its packaging, will lose value over a year. Schools, therefore, must estimate the value of such items bearing this in mind. Depreciation is the term used to refer to the loss in value caused by age, use or both. Usually depreciation is calculated on a fixed basis: if it is estimated that the useful life of the computer equipment is five years, then the value of that computer equipment will be reduced on successive annual balance sheets to reflect that depreciation. Perhaps it would be reduced in value by 20 percent per year. Other factors such as resale value could affect that figure. In the case of a car, for example, a substantial amount of its value is lost on the day it is bought, which makes depreciation complicated to estimate accurately.

Other complications can arise. Some assets may actually be increasing in value. For example, land (this is known as appreciation). To complicate matters further, both factors could be at work. So the value of the land could be rising while the buildings on the land are getting older and in need of repair so their value, as an asset, is depreciating.

Liabilities

These are normally on the left-hand side of the balance sheet. Liabilities refer to the costs still to be incurred on the assets; the profits of an organisation are also included on this side of the balance. Loans, mortgages, outstanding bills, leasing costs and anything else that the school owes, such as tax, make up the liabilities. Profits are included because, in a business, they also have to be paid out (to the owners / shareholders). For accounting purposes, the owners' affairs are considered separately from the affairs of a business. This will not apply in most school situations where the aim is not to make a profit.

Profit and loss account

This is an historic document which compares the difference in a business between money received from selling goods and services (revenue) and costs incurred in running the operation (expenditure) over a set period. The profit and loss account is an in-depth look at one part of the balance sheet. It gives an indication of the operation's performance but is still only part of the picture. It is possible to have a healthy profit and loss account but the overall picture could be poor. The profit and loss account tells managers that if the net worth of the business over the period has increased, then there is a profit. If it has decreased, then there is a loss.

Budgets

A budget is, usually, an annual plan for the financial progress of a business. There are a number of forms of budget with the most common one being a profit budget. This seeks to predict the content of the profit and loss account and the trading pattern for any business. Other types of budget include the manpower budget (or head count budget) which seeks to anticipate the 'people costs', and the capital budget, which focuses on those items which do not generate revenue. While a profit budget might have limited applications in a school the other two have very clear implications in schools which are either growing or contracting.

Budgets provide a financial basis for planning operations. They seek to evaluate management plans and set targets for financial performance. By definition they tend to be the best estimate that can be made with the information available. As a result, they provide the means by which a senior teacher can compare the actual performance against the forecasts, and change expectations in the light of experience.

Actual performance, of course, seldom matches the forecast. There will always be factors that could not have been anticipated or which have an unexpected effect. In these circumstances, the value of having a budget is that it gives an early warning when things are going to be substantially different from the expected, and this provides time for corrective action to be taken.

Costing and finance case studies

The purpose of these case studies is to focus on the financial implications of managing a school. Examine the issues raised in the light of the school's current practice and reflect on the implications arising for financial management.

As in all theoretic case studies additional information would be needed to make decisions. Here, the detail of the actual figures would also be needed. The answers will be determined by the financial practices of the school, and whether or not it has developed a commercial ethos. The analysis will, however, give senior teachers some guidance as to the factors being sought or possible answers to the questions.

CASE STUDY 5.1

There is a limited amount of money for new resources in the school. There are two department heads who feel that their department needs a substantial amount of money invested if they are to able to deliver the curriculum successfully. There is not enough to give both what they say they need. Both heads of department believe that it is their department which should have the resources / new equipment. They both argue that their department makes the largest contribution to the school's reputation and league table performance.

What financial factors should be taken into account when comparing the rival claims of both departments?

Analysis

The answer to this, as long as the comparison is purely financial, is relatively straightforward. It is a question of comparing like with like. If they both have the same number of staff, paid on the same rates, using the same equipment / resources then the difference is based on the outcomes between each department. If, however, any or all of these are different, the simplest way to compare is to set costs against output.

Generally, it is not that simple. The choice of the time period for comparison could give a very good or a very bad result from either department. Any big, unusual expenditure will distort the figures, as would particularly good or bad examination results.

Differences in operating conditions will also have a bearing. For example, the costs of teaching in an academic subject will normally be lower than in a practical one. A direct comparison will always favour the academic subject.

In most cases the best approach is for both senior teachers to agree a basis for comparison. Otherwise, the figures could be manipulated to prove anything that anyone wanted them to.

While costs will probably be part of the analysis, care must be taken. Performance is seldom as simple as a set of figures on a page. This argument, however, relates to the use made of the figures rather than their intrinsic value. It is important to have an objective means of comparison and, providing it is realised that no calculation can tell the whole story, then the school will have a valuable basis for measuring performance of both individuals and departments.

CASE STUDY 5.2

Five senior staff members have been meeting to develop new procedures and approaches to work. You believe that the meetings have been valuable in promoting better teamwork. This, in turn, will contribute to the performance of the school.

One of the problems the group has been addressing has been work which overlaps the traditional boundaries between departments. This type of work has been a source of problems in the past, with jobs having been badly done or not done at all because they fell between two departments' responsibilities.

Other members of staff have argued that the meetings are a costly waste of time. There are no additional, direct costs but indirectly the time of the five is a cost.

You would like to evaluate the exercise in financial terms to see whether the costs do justify the benefits. What financial factors would you take into account to make this judgement?

Analysis

There are many reasons why it is of value to have a means of measuring the output of such a series of meetings against their costs.

There are no **additional** costs to the school. However, the costs that exist already are still very real. The simplest way is to estimate the cost of paying the people. This could be done on the basis of the length of the meetings or the amount of time away from the work place and some additional estimate could be made of the amount of time spent outside the meetings on work arising.

This could be difficult to estimate since some of the time may have been spent on those items whether the meetings had taken place or not. Other costs could relate to the room used and whether there were costs incurred relating to heat, light and refreshments that would not otherwise have been incurred.

The benefits are more difficult to estimate and the approach is to try to use some standard way to estimate this. For example, increasing enrolment (under formula funding it will be particularly easy to measure the benefits of this financially) or reducing duplication of effort. In some cases, these benefits can be easily demonstrated in savings. If the benefits of the meetings are to stop problems from arising, then the estimate of financial benefits becomes more speculative. 'If we had not taken action, we would have lost that group of pupils and that would have lost us £X, in revenue.' This type of estimate is valuable, but of necessity is open to challenge.

From a human point of view, if the benefits of such an exercise can be demonstrated, it does tend to make a senior teacher's case stronger.

In a school context, it is more likely that the educational benefits will carry more weight but financial benefits are becoming more important as schools take increasing responsibility for their own budgets.

CASE STUDY 5.3

You have just been given information on the financial performance of your school or department. It is now six months since the start of the year and your costs are much higher than forecast. There were a number of unanticipated problems and you have had to pay / buy extra to ensure that the work is done, but the increased costs are not matched by increased performance.

The initial forecast was based on figures given by you and were the best estimate that you could make at the time. To stay within budget you could cut back on the range of subjects offered by your department. This would have no effect on this year's income but would reduce the income to the school next year. In the long run this would probably cause the school difficulty in competing for pupils with other schools in the area.

What costs might you be able to be cut back, without affecting the work of your school / department?

What would the longer term costs (if any) of such cost savings be? In this case you may wish to include non-financial costs (e.g. poor examination results).

Analysis

Having been a party to the development of the budget the senior teacher now has to stand by the estimates given. While this may not be entirely fair it is frequently necessary. A department which has overspent its budget or under-performed, in terms of revenue generation may have a series of legitimate reasons but financial realities mean that some changes are going to have to be made.

In many situations, improvement can only come about from generating additional revenue. Only so much can be cut back without affecting the operation directly. Then certain basic costs are left and these will remain more or less the same

whatever the level of activity. However, for the purposes of this exercise senior teachers have been asked to identify those costs within their own operation that they could reduce without directly affecting the operation.

The most common way of doing this is to reduce spending on items that do not have a direct or immediate effect on operations.

For example, in difficult times, staff training is often cut. This does not have an immediate effect, in fact in the short term it might actually improve performance by saving the time spent on staff training and using it productively. In the longer term, however, it is, usually, detrimental to the operation. The restriction on the development of the employees can result in a skill shortage at a later date but also can affect the motivation of employees. In particular, the ambitious employee may see this in very negative terms. The cost of lost motivation can be difficult to calculate unless it shows up in a direct way such as an increase in employee turnover. That can be calculated on the basis of the costs of recruitment and the training of new employees.

There are other ways of reducing costs, for example, holding lower stocks of books, materials or other equipment. If the stock were too high to start with, very real savings can be made. It does beg the question, however, as to why this was allowed to happen.

The answer is likely to be specific to the individual school and department.

CASE STUDY 5.4

You have recently taken over the running of a school or department. There has been some dissatisfaction with the way that this school or department was managed in the past, and there is a clear expectation that things will improve under you. Dissatisfaction seems to have centred on poor academic performance, stated simply, the examination performance when matched to the staff and resources allocated has been very poor.

You have made a few initial observations and it would seem that the problem is one of different work commitment among staff members. The efforts and work done by some staff is barely adequate while others are clearly putting in time and effort beyond what could be reasonably expected.

A further problem relates to the staff. Some seem to believe that the value of their work far exceeds the actual value. They seem to believe that the income generated by the school for the pupils they teach is much higher than it actually is. This has resulted in an attitude which at times seems to verge on: 'When you put the money that my classes generate for the school against what they actually pay me, I am being robbed by the school.'

What financial information would be of value to you in this situation?

How could you use this information as part of your approach to improving the overall performance of the school or department?

Analysis

The problems are arguably much deeper than finance in this case study. However, objective information on performance could be part of the answer. The employees need to be given accurate feedback on their performance. They are doing this themselves to some extent, but are over-estimating their own worth.

An employer has substantial costs relating to staff apart from those that are paid to the person in wages (National Insurance contribution, sick pay, materials and equipment, heat, light, etc. all add to the costs of employing a person). The calculation by staff also certainly does not take into account waste of time or materials, the cost of providing management supervision and administrative back-up.

To look at the other side, the per pupil income from formula funding will not give an accurate guide either. A series of other costs will be incurred including administration, caretaking, building and equipment maintenance to name only a few. As always the actual detail will vary from one school to another.

Clear performance indicators for employees with realistic targets could be the first steps back towards an improved and more consistent performance of this department. However, if these could be shown to have a sound financial basis then that will increase their credibility.

Organisational aspects

Many problems can be avoided through careful planning and organisation. This is true for schools and departments of all sizes but, as in most things, the bigger the numbers the bigger the scope for problems. Solving overall organisational problems is often seen as the sole responsibility of the principal or senior teachers. Clearly the co-operation of all staff in addressing such problems will mean better solutions in most cases. Good financial management is not merely about figures. Good management of the people will have major benefits to the financial health of the school.

Situations where there is most likely to be a problem and where costs may be incurred unnecessarily are varied and include:

- The system for identifying staff absence and responding appropriately to it.

- The means by which new staff are inducted into the school's ways.

- Consistent agreed approaches to common disciplinary problems among staff, e.g. poor performance, disruptive behaviour, lateness, persistent absence. Schools usually do this for pupils. It may also be an important issue to address in relation to staff.

- A system to ensure that the work of absent staff is quickly identified and covered.

- The system for monitoring performance and responding to problems at an early stage.

- The means by which common problems can be identified and agreed action taken.

- Vague budget items that can account for a significant part of costs.

There are always a number of these problems occurring in any school. To tackle them all at the same time is not realistic. However, it is also generally true that most problems tend to come from a small number of sources. An approach to focusing on the most important problems or those which will give the best return for your efforts is outlined later.

Staff involvement

Virtually all organisations emphasise the need for the involvement of staff. However, this sometimes means little more than a pious, or worse still, cynical statement. That is probably unfair to many schools who do make genuine efforts to consult and involve staff in decision making. It should also be noted that the situation has improved in recent years. However, it is still the rare organisation that genuinely consults its staff prior to taking decisions that have financial implications rather than informing them after the event.

The views of staff, like those of senior teachers can be very wide-ranging. In some cases they can have strongly held but ill-informed views on issues. While it is unrealistic to expect people to have total commitment to a policy which they have no input into formulating, it is equally unrealistic to expect that every employee can have her full say in every issue involving investment or expenditure.

The challenge for schools is to find a way to consult genuinely while retaining the confidence of staff and their own decision-making power. Any decisions made must have the full confidence of senior teachers , since they will, of course, have to implement them.

Organisations have tried a number of approaches. Meetings of the entire work force have some value. However, not everyone will attend such a meeting and even less will be willing to talk in front of a large group. The views expressed tend to structure the outcome and these will reflect the actual views of a very small minority. Small group briefing session are probably more successful in garnering the views of employees. However, it is does take time to build confidence in such an approach.

There is often the added difficulty of non-teaching staff in schools feeling that their views are less valid than those of qualified teachers.

Any system will have drawbacks. The important point is that staff have an opportunity to have their views heard prior to the implementation of decisions that affect what they do, and that their individual circumstances are listened to if a problem arises.

The issue of staff consultation is really about attitude towards their views. If the only time senior teachers talk or listen to staff is when they want staff help and support because the school is in financial difficulty, then expect little loyalty and commitment to management's plans.

In recent years people have become very aware of their rights and will resist anyone who they believe is denying them their rights. Equally, many employees will be afraid to say anything derogatory. They are aware that the goodwill of their managers will be critical to their employment in the school.

In a customer-care context it is sometimes stated that, for every complaint made, there are up to twenty others who say nothing but are equally dissatisfied. While the relationship between employer and staff is not that of a supplier and customer, it has certain aspects in common. And the numbers who actually complain are probably similar in proportion.

At all times, the issue is one of approach and attitude. If staff, particularly non-teaching staff, are treated as a necessary inconvenience then they will generally react in the same way. If they are only consulted when there is a problem, their loyalty to the school will be determined by how much management's views and theirs coincide. If their view of the school is largely a negative one, based mainly on a lack of respect for their opinions, then to expect enthusiasm or anything more than basic support is unrealistic. If they are frightened of senior teachers as authority figures then the support given will depend on whether that fear is based on respect or contempt.

Staff involvement is not a simple issue but the following approaches have been used:

- Prior to finalising decisions which will have an impact on working practices, survey staff views, either by use of a questionnaire or through small group meetings. This will give staff the opportunity to express views. A brief overview of the results of the questionnaire (or discussions) and how their views were incorporated into the final decision could then be fed back.

- When informing employees of any changes and new investments and expenditure, give reasons and outline the benefits to the school and to them.

- Structured methods of communication are important, e.g. a staff notice board and staff briefing meetings. However, do not assume that these are enough. Genuine communication is difficult, it is a two-way process. Formal methods tend to allow the school to tell staff about issues but allow for limited feedback.

- To ensure consistency, an agreed set of situations in which staff should be informed and involved should be agreed among management, otherwise, it becomes a matter of chance. These are often issues such as the implementation of change, but management might also wish to consider involving the staff on a wider range of issues.

6: Managing information

Introduction

Within all working situations there is a wide range of information available. Not all of this information is relevant to decision making. Choosing what to record and keep and what to discard should be based on a thorough knowledge of the school, its aims and purposes. Once this is understood, performance indicators and measures can be realistically evaluated.

This chapter focuses initially on the evaluation of priorities and then seeks to develop this theme in terms of the values and principles by which the school is run. Arguably, these issues could have been addressed earlier in the book. The topics are all connected and it is possible to argue that any point is the start. The issues are raised here because it is easier to consider them in more depth with the background in the other areas to draw from.

Principles and values case studies

The following case studies are designed to highlight the priorities within the school through looking at possible situations. It is important in your answers to emphasise the exchange of information between individuals and departments as the basis for problem solving.

As always, it is better to discuss your answers with a group; however, if this option is not open to you, discuss them with at least one other person. This will help to highlight issues and give the topic a proper airing. It also tends to result in better answers.

The detail given is not enough in itself to make a decision about what you would actually do. However, the case studies do raise real problems and you may wish to use them to help you make decisions about your actions.

CASE STUDY 6.1

There have been some problems of motivation within staff at the school. There is an off-hand attitude towards work. The view that 'it's good enough' is fairly common. The school is not under any immediate threat. However, this will not remain true if the attitude being expressed persists.

You have challenged individuals on this and they have backed down and agreed with you. However, you know that this change of mind is not real. Once out of your presence their work will be done well enough to keep them out of trouble, but no better. Your main concern is the complacency that underlies this attitude. People express the pride they have in their work and in doing a good job. But, when examined, this is not demonstrated by what they actually do.

It would seem that some senior staff share this view. They believe that there is nothing wrong and that as the school is not under any threat you are panicking needlessly. In your view, you are justifiably concerned about the long-term future. It is difficult to put your finger on a specific example. The vast majority of staff do their work well enough to meet the basic requirements of the job.

What is lacking is that extra edge that you believe is important. What should the school and / or you as an individual senior teacher do in this situation?

Analysis

Strictly speaking, staff are doing their job so it could be argued that there is no problem here. However, most senior teachers and schools want more than that and the long-term future of any school depends on its employees giving more than the bare minimum.

The question is more one of motivation and encouragement than of discipline. How can staff be made feel part of the school, that their interests lie with the success of the school? Any approach which emphasises communication, involvement and which focuses on improving motivation will be important here.

CASE STUDY 6.2

The teacher in the classroom beside yours is clearly having problems controlling pupils. He is a relatively new teacher who contributes confidently to staff discussions of most issues. As far as you are aware, no one else knows that there are problems.

There are a number of other problems in other parts of the school which are probably masking this one. Your concern is that it is unlikely to come to the principal's attention for some time, in which case the consequences are likely to be very serious for this teacher, since the damage done will have been going on for a long period. There is also a possibility that other senior teachers, including you, will be blamed for not noticing and doing something to resolve the problem.

It would seem that pupils are being allowed to do pretty much as they please. If your colleague tries to impose his will, they listen for a moment but carry on as before.

You have enquired about how the teacher feels he is coping but have been given no insight into the problems. The teacher says either that the department is doing well or makes light of any difficulties. You think that he may be concerned at the loss of face should others find out about the problems. However, you know matters are getting worse.

There is an increasing note of desperation and pleading in this teacher's voice whenever he addresses an individual or the whole class. Even at some distance this is clearly detectable. In these circumstances what, if anything, should you do to help?

Analysis

In one respect, it could be said that this is none of your business. You have fulfilled your duty by making a general enquiry, your offer of help has been rejected, what else can you do? However, the other question that needs to be answered is what you would want to happen if you were the teacher having problems. Most teachers say that they would like help, as long as it would not take away from their position or authority. This is an impossible answer. If you intervene then you are taking away something from the teacher. Conversely, he has already lost much of his position and authority.

The case study highlights one of the problems of leaving all disciplinary matters in the hands of the individual teacher. As long as everyone can cope that approach works but when problems arises there is no mechanism to either identify the problem or to intervene in a helpful way.

CASE STUDY 6.3

You are concerned about one of the most 'difficult' members of staff in the school. Her job involves work in a number of different departments and while, in theory, she reports to one of the senior teachers, in reality there is little control exercised. There are frequent complaints from teachers and others about this person's attitude even though the quality of her work is good.

The work this person does is specialised and necessary and she is good at the job but difficult to work with. She is openly critical about matters that are of no concern to her. More seriously, because she works in a number of departments, she will prioritise work to her own desires rather than to its importance. You have tried to speak both to this person and the senior teacher she reports to. However, you have not had much success in this. There is a tendency to point to the quality of the work done and say that relationship problems are a two-way issue. Following from this, she has complained about the behaviour and attitudes of various members of your staff.

You know that the people involved are not difficult to work with but may well have behaved unreasonably when faced with the attitude of this individual. Other teachers will privately express the same problems with this person but have not complained to her, or her senior teacher. How can you best approach this in order to maximise co-operation from all the staff involved with this employee?

Analysis

There are a number of approaches that you could take within your own department to minimise problems. Undoubtedly, these problems would be better handled by a common, consistent approach from all senior teachers and with the co-operation of the senior teacher responsible for the person.

The case study gives another example of the problems that can arise when there is no overall policy and strategy. This type of problem is more common where the difficult individual has expertise or skills which make her job necessary and beyond the understanding of the teachers for whom she does the work. In some cases, even the senior teacher this person reports to may not be as 'technically' knowledgeable as she.

A further angle on the problem is the view of the person causing the problems. A senior teacher who genuinely understands her point of view, is more likely to be able to resolve the issue. However, the lack of a common approach is the principal problem here.

CASE STUDY 6.4

While relations between staff at all levels are generally good, you have noticed some dissatisfaction being expressed recently. There is no single complaint but you feel that a significant number have disagreements with the school in how it is conducting its affairs. Some feel that the staff's opinions about work-related matters are not being taken seriously enough. Others complain that they are having difficulty keeping up with the volume of work expected, while others have expressed the view that the 'rewards' for work done are not being shared fairly.

There are plenty of similar jobs elsewhere should staff choose to leave. This has not been a major problem, to date, but if it were to happen would be of major concern.

There are mixed views from the senior teachers on the matter. Many feel that the staff simply do not understand what management are trying to achieve and that as their views are contradictory there is little they could do about it in any case.

Others are very concerned that the complaints they are hearing are the 'tip of the iceberg' and that the problem is a serious one of loss of confidence in the school by the staff. They are worried that this, in turn, will lead to a withdrawal of support for the school in matters such as out-of-school activities and flexibility. How should the school address this issue?

Analysis

This case study is focused on the role, rights and responsibilities of staff. At one time, it was generally believed that the manager's or senior teacher's job was to come up with all the good ideas and that the views of the 'work force' were irrelevant. This is no longer commonly held as a belief and, in addition, people are now much more vocal in their views.

Clearly, senior teachers have the right and responsibility to pursue the work of their department in the manner that they believe is best. However, this is not an open invitation to do as they please. Staff should at least be communicated with, and preferably, involved in developing the school. That would seem to be the main problem in this example. Telling employees what you are doing may not change their minds but if the communication is genuine (i.e. two-way) then you will have the understanding of the work force and are more likely to get their support.

Problem solving

Perhaps one of the major sources of frustration for managers in any sector is that the causes of problems and low standards seem to be beyond either their control or that of the organisation. In some cases, their actions appear to make no substantial difference to the situation and, as long as that situation exists, improvement will be unlikely. In some cases, these problems are serious and in no way related to the operation of the organisation. That does not, however, lessen their effect upon standards. These are the problems which require more in-depth investigation and a structured and co-ordinated approach to their resolution.

One of the most commonly quoted examples of this is 'poor' intake of pupils. However well-managed the school is, if the pupils have serious problems on arrival or if the school is under-resourced then it is difficult to improve performance.

In such circumstances, it can be difficult to be motivated enough to put in the effort necessary to raise standards. It would be foolish to try to pretend that senior teachers can always change things. A further frustration could be that teachers may still be held accountable for the lack of achievement.

In most situations, however, organisations can influence events even when they cannot control them. It is often said that there are no problems, only opportunities. While it is easy to be cynical about a statement like this, there is some truth in it. Some of the best developments arise out of what was originally perceived to be a problem.

It has been demonstrated that a structured approach to problem solving is particularly beneficial with these types of difficulties. Four of the more commonly used approaches to problem solving form the focus of this section. The techniques outlined also have value in addressing problems originating within the organisation.

Problem-solving techniques should be simple to apply and help in the identification and analysis of problems. However, before these can be of value, the first step is for someone to accept ownership of the problem. In the types of problems being discussed, this is the most difficult step. If no one sees the problem as belonging to them they will not put the time and effort into resolving it.

Telling others what they should do will usually not be an effective substitute. However, resolution will often depend on working co-operatively with others.

Problem-solving techniques
Brain storming

This is probably the most popular and best known of the techniques. It is based on the assumption that the best solutions tend to come when one individual can spark off ideas in another. Any group that sits down to discuss and resolve a problem could be called a brain-storming group. However, the technique is most successful if the following format is adhered to:

- The problem should be stated as a short and easily understood proposition. For example, 'In how many ways can we improve examination performance?'

- Group members should be encouraged to produce as many ideas as possible during the brain-storming stage. It can be useful to set a target, for example, twenty ideas in fifteen minutes.

- No evaluation of the ideas should take place during that phase. Encourage odd or unusual ideas. They may not in themselves be practical but it is often from these that the most creative ideas develop.

- Group members should be given time to prepare individually before the session starts.

- There is usually an initial burst of ideas, then they tend to dry up. It can be tempting at that stage to stop. But the best ideas often come after this quiet period.

- The ideas should be recorded briefly in a place where all group members can see them. A flip chart or chalk board usually works best.

- When all the ideas have been recorded then evaluation can begin. If it starts during the session, it will inhibit people. Sometimes the best ideas come from what was initially a joke or a cynical remark, so *all* ideas should be recorded.

- It is often better if evaluation focuses initially on ruling out the impractical, those the organisation has no control over and in grouping similar ideas.

- The final step is deciding which to try first. One way of doing this is after the impractical has been ruled out and the similar grouped, then define the criteria for the solution. The ideas which conform most closely to those criteria are the 'best'.

A brain storming group can be of any size but the best solutions tend to come from those groups which are between five and twelve in number. Any smaller and the range of ideas is restricted. Any bigger and it is unlikely that everyone will contribute. If the group is larger than this, it is better to split it into a number of smaller groups for brain storming as this tends to increase the effectiveness of the exercise. Each small group should bring back three or four broad solutions to the main group. These can then be discussed and evaluated.

Pareto Analysis

This technique was briefly referred to earlier. Pareto was an Italian economist who devised a theory about the distribution of wealth. Stated simply, he proposed that 80 percent of the wealth of a country was owned by 20 percent of its citizens. This is sometimes called the 80:20 Rule and seems to apply in a surprisingly wide number of situations.

In the context of people management, by Pareto's rule 80 percent of problems would come from 20 percent of the staff (e.g. in a department of ten two staff members would cause most problems). The same is true in the positive: 80 percent of the achievement of the department will come from 20 percent of the employees. Whether the percentages hold true precisely is questionable. However, the broad principles of Pareto Analysis do work.

Take the reduction of disciplinary problems as an example. If there are five major causes of disciplinary problems in a school, Pareto Analysis would indicate that most problems will be the result of one of those causes. If a senior teacher tries to resolve all five at the same time, success is unlikely due to dissipation of effort. If, however, the one or two most important causes are focused on, there is more hope of making a real difference.

As a result of a review of the school's or department's procedures and performance, there may be many suggestions as to how matters might be improved. Pareto Analysis would suggest that out of twenty suggestions, four would have the biggest impact. Four is a manageable number of initiatives to handle.

To use Pareto Analysis properly it is necessary to measure and keep records. Often senior teachers' impressions about the frequency of particular problems bear little relationship to reality. They may take more notice of a problem that causes inconvenience and is easily attributed at the time than to a problem that does not have such an obvious or immediate effect.

Analysis of causes

Many problems have complex causes and are, therefore, difficult to resolve. This technique encourages managers to examine the contributory factors under a series of headings. This can help simplify the problem and make the approach to resolution more logical. In an industrial setting, this approach often divides the problem into contributory factors associated with machinery, people, procedures and materials. Clearly these would not apply in a school context.

In a school, this analysis could be translated into pupils, curriculum, procedures, staff and resources. Procedures refers to the school's rules and ways of doing things. Additional factors might be added which relate to specific areas that are important in particular circumstances. The categories under which the headings are defined will vary from one situation to another.

Once the major causes of the problem have been identified it is common to do a further similar analysis on those. The contributory factors to those causes are examined under the same headings. By the time that second level of analysis is complete, most of the factors will have been examined and discussed so a further level of analysis will not usually be productive.

Performance banding

This technique also had its initial applications in industrial settings. It has more recently been used in service organisations but would seem also to have applications to schools. It is best defined as an early warning system, using minor problems to establish patterns and to indicate where preventative action should be taken.

The technique is based on the assumption that there are standards to which all aspects of the school's activities should conform. It is the lack of conformance which is at the root of any problems. The means of resolving this type of problem in an industrial setting has sometimes been to set up complex monitoring systems, followed by statistical analysis of the results. The technique described here has some aspects in common with that but is a simpler approach and more suited to a school environment.

First, the assumption must be accepted that problems arise when what actually happens does not conform to pre-set standards. Then even a minor variation, while not a problem in itself, can be an early warning sign of problems to come. If action is taken, it will save the need for further more serious action later and prevent a real problem from occurring.

In order to operate this system detailed analysis of the processes to be monitored is needed. The term 'processes' can cover virtually anything that happens in the school from academic results and the incidence of disciplinary problems to specific aspects such as time keeping and attendance. Because of the work involved setting up the system of performance banding, it is really only practical in a situation where there is a major problem or where a significant change is being planned.

Having identified the problem or area to be focused on, the first step is to decide on a series of bands or levels of performance. School staff should define these. One unusual aspect is, that once the level is defined, any variation (even an improvement) should be investigated. If, for example, the process focused on was pupil attendance, having decided the performance bands any variation, good or bad, should be reacted to.

These decisions on bands of performance are best based on historical data. If these do not exist, then the first step is to set the systems in place which will gather them. The more accurate and real this information is, the more useful it will be in setting performance bands. Be careful of setting standards which are simply wishful thinking. That will lead to frustration.

The precise settings of bands will often vary over time (the day, week or year). In monitoring pupil attendance, for example, the level set for the first weeks of term might be very different from what would be expected in the last weeks of the school year. In addition, the performance bands for different year groups or classes may be different.

Two sets of defining parameters are needed: a narrow band which defines where the school wants the performance to be; a broad band which defines the outer limits of acceptable performance. It takes some adjustment in the early stages to get these parameters right. The notion of accepting a less than perfect performance also takes some getting used to. However, the objective is to improve the standards over a long period, so perfection does still have its place. The standards defined are always capable of being redefined in the light of changing circumstances.

The next stage is monitoring. Any variation from the narrow band of performance is worthy of note, and consistent breaches require investigation. The nature of this investigation tends to depend on whether the variation is in the 'right' or the 'wrong' direction. Both should be examined in a similar way but the 'bad' variation will usually be taken more seriously. However, identifying the reasons for an unexpected improvement can help improve overall standards as much as identifying problems and remedying those.

In investigating a variation, it is important to try to look behind the immediate reasons, to try to ascertain why they should cause a change. As already stated, any variation should be examined but a full-scale investigation tends to happen only when breaches of the narrow band occur consistently.

Defining 'consistently' in this context is difficult without a concrete example to work from. However, as a rule of thumb, four breaches of the narrow band within a defined period (usually a week) is commonly used. This does need to be interpreted in the light of what is being monitored. Any breach of the broad band requires a full investigation.

Results are often charted in graph form so that variations from the expected are visible and patterns become immediately obvious. In addition, if the actual settings of the bands vary (i.e. expected performance levels are not always the same) this is also obvious. On a day-to-day basis, a manager or senior teacher can see at a glance both where performance should be and where it actually is.

As already stated, the objective is to raise standards over a longer period. It is not a quick or an easy fix. The approach also carries the danger of complacency. As long as performance stays within the narrow band, it can seem that there is no cause for concern. This attitude is totally at odds with the purpose of performance banding – it is a technique which enables managers to improve, based on a careful examination and review of performance data.

There has been no attempt to give an exhaustive list of problem-solving techniques. As should have become clear, they tend not to solve problems, rather they are ways of helping managers to analyse and prioritise and thus they do help in decision making. Solving problems requires effort and commitment – no technique will relieve managers of that.

7: Raising standards of staff performance

Introduction

This chapter comprises a series of case studies focusing on the difficult aspects of managing members of staff. The first set relates to the difficult issues in dealing with problems of low performance among staff. Readers are asked to consider, in particular, the training implications of the problems. In addition, there is a whole school developmental aspect. What help and support would the reader like to be available when situations like this actually occur? Analysis of each case study is provided which seeks to highlight some of the issues involved but does not prescribe answers. This is the task for the senior teachers.

This is followed by some general points on how to raise the performance of all staff. The emphasis here is on those members of staff who do not present any problems as such. The general principles have an application to all staff but may have to be adapted when working with those whose knowledge, level of skill or motivation results in additional support being needed.

Raising performance case studies
Case study 7.1

June is a well-liked member of staff. On paper she is well-qualified but her whole approach to work is inefficient. She never really follows through on anything and as a result there is plenty of evidence of her starting a project but, on many occasions, it is abandoned when her interest is taken with something else.

If asked June will always have a good reason for having changed direction. This will always seem reasonable and logical. But the number and frequency of these changes mean that too many things are left unfinished. Sometimes others will 'pick up the pieces'. This has probably masked the real extent of the problem. Because June is well-liked no one really complains.

June will also offer to do anything that needs to be done, however unrelated to her job. Again, this willingness tends to disarm people. June is also very good at 'pulling things together' at short notice. This has been useful when you have been under pressure from outsiders. However, even here, once you look past the good presentation, it is obvious that there is little substance in what has been done and that in turn tends to mean that somebody has to put the real work in later without any acknowledgement.

How could a senior teacher best help June?

On a whole school basis, how could help and support for staff whose performance is barely adequate be best directed?

Analysis

Earlier chapters have focused on the need for review and monitoring and that is clearly what is needed here. Staff like June are often good at judging just how much is needed and giving only that.

The problem is just as likely to be one of management as to do with June herself. It would seem that she responds well to the pressure of the moment. If that is so it would seem that the management style has been to let people work unsupervised until an outsider makes a direct demand and then to pass that on to staff. As a manager, your demands on June need to be quite specific and need to be reviewed and monitored so that June gets regular, frequent and detailed feedback on her performance.

At a whole school level, if June is involved in a team project, careful thought will need to be given to her role. June has undoubted gifts, she is good at presentation and she may also be quite creative but she does not seem to be good at finishing work. Careful planning on the composition of groups will mean that her strengths can be maximised and balanced with those of others.

CASE STUDY 7.2

Clare is one of the most difficult members of staff to handle. She is aggressive and bad tempered but works extremely hard and is among the highest performing staff. She has few friends among the other staff but her work and achievements are generally respected.

Because her work commitment is so high, she is quite well-thought of in the school, and numerous attempts have been made by you and others to build some kind of working relationship with Clare. However, all these attempts have failed.

Her attitude towards anyone in management borders on contempt. She is not a good team member but will do any work assigned to her. If she has to work co-operatively with others they usually complain afterwards about how difficult she was to work with.

Your belief is that Clare is a perfectionist and has no respect for anyone who does not live up to her standards. Unfortunately, this includes the rest of the school's staff. While there are no problems with Clare's own work, it is very difficult to encourage teamwork with Clare. Arguably, Clare has no performance problems but your efforts to improve the performance generally are being hampered by her behaviour.

How can you, as senior teacher, best handle staff like this in the context of an attempt to improve teamwork?

What are the implications for the whole school of high-performing individuals who do not work well in teams?

Analysis

This is one of the most common problems of teamwork. How do you handle the high-performing individual who destroys teamwork in the rest of the team? If you are genuinely convinced of the benefits of teamwork then Clare's behaviour will not be accepted. Depending on circumstances, it could even have a disciplinary aspect to it. Most principals and senior teachers would find this difficult to implement in a real situation.

It is likely that you depend to some degree on Clare's performance. Trying to change this is trying to kill the 'goose which lays the golden eggs'. It is quite likely, therefore, that Clare's behaviour has been inadvertently encouraged, at least insofar as her high level of performance has been acknowledged.

Unless you are willing to integrate Clare into the team, you are not going to improve performance in this way. As in some of the other cases, it is very likely that Clare does not recognise her behaviour as a problem. The first step may be to alert her to this. But it is important that this problem is tackled.

At another level you need to try to measure the detrimental effect Clare's behaviour is having on others. This may change the manner in which her behaviour is viewed. You may find that the person you thought was delivering a good individual performance was, in fact, partly responsible for an overall low performance.

Without further detail it is difficult to know how justified Clare's attitudes are. It is possible that her behaviour is justifiable given the previous circumstances. However, it is also probably true that unless you can change that, behaviour performance will not improve any further.

CASE STUDY 7.3

Richard is a quiet, almost withdrawn teacher. He copes well with his classes where his quiet style seems to be effective. However, at meetings he would not challenge or disagree with another teacher, and rarely contributes to staff meetings, and when he does it will only be in answer to a direct question.

While this does not cause any direct problems, you feel that Richard does have a lot contribute to current developments in the school. You feel that you are not getting the best from this teacher in a group situation. In addition, you do have some concerns about his teaching. Richard has his own ways of doing things. Changes in teaching methods seem to make little difference to the way he teaches. No direct problems have arisen because of this but other teachers are complaining that taking a class that Richard has taught is difficult. There will be areas not covered and gaps in knowledge.

In particular, any recent changes in the curriculum will not have been covered and it is fairly clear that Richard is not even attempting to change in response to these. You are concerned not so much that Richard lacks the ability to teach or understand the changes but that his isolation from other teachers results in his not entirely understanding changes and, as a result, taking longer to implement them.

How could a senior teacher best approach this problem?

How could the training and development efforts of the school be best co-ordinated to help this type of employee?

Analysis

A teacher like this would probably not have presented as a problem twenty or even ten years ago. While there were changes to the curriculum, they tended to be more slowly introduced. His lack of contribution at staff meetings would have been seen in many schools as a good thing. There were always more than enough teachers asking difficult questions and voicing their opinions, so a quiet one was often welcomed.

However, if we accept the model of teamwork as being the best way forward, then the failure to contribute does become a problem. Of course, just because someone does not speak at a staff meeting does not mean that they are not contributing. The real problem with Richard would seem to be that he is not involved in the developments at any level and does not appear to be making any attempt to become involved. His abilities to influence a class would indicate that he is capable of making a quiet but effective contribution.

It may be that you have to find a way for this teacher to become involved. It may also be that his quietness masks his distaste for the changes that are being made. The issue would then be one of motivation. The failure to implement changes to the curriculum is particularly worrying. It could be a failure to understand the nature of those changes, it could be a difficulty in adapting to new situations or it could be a form of passive resistance to change.

Careful analysis is needed before deciding on a course of action for Richard. This should try to ensure that he becomes more involved in the changes and that the contribution expected is appropriate for him.

CASE STUDY 7.4

You have been managing Tom for some years. Initially, you thought that he simply lacked ability. He appears uninterested in promotion but his work is done passably well most of the time.

When Tom is interested or motivated his work suddenly improves; he puts in extra hours, contributes to the work of teams in the department / school and appears to be highly competent. However, the number of times that Tom has appeared interested are very small.

Training courses on new developments have improved Tom's performance. However, this does not last long. It is difficult to point to anything specific that Tom has done badly. It is just that you believe that he is capable of better and he has demonstrated this occasionally. Tom's general attitude and approach to work, while not enthusiastic, do not give any cause for concern.

What could a senior teacher do to improve Tom's performance?

How should the school's training resources and management efforts be co-ordinated to ensure staff like this perform better?

Analysis

In most cases like this, the member of staff is not trying to perform to the expected level. In many cases he does not even know what the expected level is. If asked to rate their own performance people like Tom often show no indication of recognising that there is a problem. They are not breaking any rules and there is nothing actually being done wrong. It is just that you feel that they could do better. This does not seem to be a disciplinary problem, therefore.

At an individual level, Tom needs to be motivated. This could involve a series of actions from you, for example, getting Tom to set goals and objectives, training in

> *specific skills, giving additional responsibility, giving direct constructive feedback or ensuring that Tom is involved in relevant developments. There are many others. The main thrust of action should be to involve Tom and give him feedback in a way that will encourage him to take more of an interest.*
>
> *At the more general management level, the school's training resources should be aimed at doing many of the same things at a group level, teamwork training and taking on group projects being two of the more obvious.*

Analysis of these case studies is general in nature. The range and type of schools make more specific advice on a topic that may have a direct effect on people's job prospects difficult. Care should be taken here, as with all other case studies, that comments or advice given is not seen as prescriptive.

The staff that often gives the most concern to managers at a time of change are those who do the present job well enough, but are not able or willing to take on new responsibilities. In one way or another the case studies focus on the types of problems this kind of group raises.

With some it is a lack of ability, with others it is way the work is done which causes the problems. Training in these cases often focuses only on the new skills involved. However, if a senior teacher is trying to change attitudes then this, too, should be the focus for part of the training.

It may have to be accepted, however, that some staff will not be able to cope with the demands of a new situation. Decisions about such staff are extremely difficult. Often they are genuinely trying to conform to what is expected. If they are perceived to have been treated badly then a negative message will have been passed to everyone. Equally, not to take any action is tantamount to accepting that the planned changes are going to fail.

In many cases training and support will provide an answer but it may take a considerable amount of time. A further problem can relate to the team approach. It has been argued in this book that a team performance will give more scope for genuine improvement. It is on this aspect that some of the individuals in the case studies are failing and it is here that training sometimes needs to be directed. Many people are not good team players by nature, and unless encouraged and trained to work that way are unlikely to change. Teaching in particular has traditionally been an individual skill. It is unreasonable to expect teachers to change without help and support.

Whatever answers senior teachers decide are most appropriate for their school or department, having a common approach from all will enhance the likelihood of overcoming these problems.

Raising standards among better performing staff

Normally the focus for improvement is on those with the lowest performance. This is true in any situation where we seek improvement by identifying problems and then trying to remedy them. However, very real gains can be made at other levels. Normally, it is only a minority that will have serious problems but all are capable of improvement.

It could be argued that better performing staff have no need of special help, except when they run into difficulty. There are many characteristics of those with a high level of ability, probably the most striking one being the degree of independence that they have in managing change. They often appear to need no direction, except insofar as that gives them focus and motivation for their efforts. While this is true performance can still be further enhanced by various means.

Involvement in planning

It has already been argued that most people will have a stronger commitment and feel more ownership of any situation where they have had a say in the planning. Staff who understand what they are trying achieve in detail, how it is to be done and are able to monitor their progress will be better motivated than those who must blindly follow the directions given.

This approach has applications at all levels of performance but the most able staff, in particular, benefit from it. They often have the ability to structure and take control of their own output. The main difficulty tends to be in finding the mechanism for making this happen. Group approaches are possible but it is usually more effective if it is done on an individual basis. If there are a large number of tasks and staff, this exercise can be time consuming.

For each task, the outcome and criteria for successful achievement must be defined and an outline given of the time constraints and critical quality issues. This should then be discussed on a whole department (or other group) basis. The senior teacher should then discuss with each individual how that person intends to approach and plan her performance of each task. How will she know if she is performing at the expected level? How much and what type of commitment is needed from the staff member?

Target setting

In virtually any area of endeavour, performance can be raised by target or objective setting. As with planning, target setting has applications to all ability and performance levels but has particular value with those who have the ability to control and structure their own work. The concept has applications in many different settings and depends on the notion that people perform better if they have a definite, easily measured goal to aim for.

Feedback on performance

Feedback should follow naturally from planning and target setting. If someone is given knowledge of the results of his efforts and is in a position to make changes based on that knowledge, then performance will normally improve. Sometimes this improvement is simply that performance becomes more consistent. In most cases, however, very real improvements can be made by this method alone. Important aspects related to feedback to staff include:

- feedback should be given promptly (immediate feedback is the most effective)

- it must be fair and based on the employee's efforts and performance

- the effects can be enhanced if the information is accompanied by an acknowledgement of achievement and effort

- information and guidance on how poor performance could be improved can enhance the effectiveness of feedback

- it can broaden the employee's understanding and perspective of what is required

- feedback should be positive and constructive. If it is to be credible, it must be genuine. Generally, the more factual it is, the more credible it will be to the employee.

Delegation of decision-making authority

Ultimately delegation is about trust. Can the person be trusted to make decisions, regulate her own work and motivate herself. Many managers have double standards on delegation. They believe that their boss does not trust them enough but they fail to show the same trust in others. Successful delegation includes the following elements:

- It is planned.

- The limits of authority must be defined.

- The person's decisions must be backed publicly and any problems sorted privately.

- Any problems must be highlighted immediately from a problem-solving perspective.

- The means of review must be agreed in advance and that must be rigidly adhered to.

- Delegation should be done gradually with training and support as needed.

Delegation works best with more able staff. However, it should always be remembered that you can delegate authority but not responsibility. That will always remain with the manager.

Managing the managers in a school

The process of managing managers is quite simple to state:

- The school defines its goals and objectives.

- Those are translated down to departmental level and possibly even to individual level.

- Departmental goals and objectives are then set.

- These often cover an extended period of say, twelve to eighteen months.

- These goals and objectives are then broken down into shorter term objectives, for example, of a term's or month's duration. This then forms a series of steps. The resources (people, equipment and training) needed are identified. This is all agreed between the senior teacher or department head and the principal.

- The senior teacher or department head is responsible for ensuring that the objectives are achieved. The principal and vice-principal are responsible for ensuring that the person has the needed support and resources to make achievement possible.

- There is a regular meeting between the more senior and other managers to review progress towards the objectives of that month, progress towards the longer term objectives and to set objectives for the coming month.

The process encourages managers to focus on a number of key performance goals and to ensure that their efforts are integrated with senior management's plans for the whole school.

The process depends on having a broader picture or vision of where the school hopes to go and a set of long-term aims to support that.

Managing staff by focusing on key objectives

Much has been written on the subject of managing by objectives, and the topic underlies much of modern management thinking. The outcome of the process is the production and regular review of a series of key departmental objectives which contribute demonstrably to the improvement of the school. However, in order to achieve this process it should help senior teachers to be able to:

- Identify a clear vision and direction for the future development of the school. In particular, they should be able to identify the level of departmental performance which demonstrates achievement at the highest levels.

- Reflect realistically on the organisation's and their own department's strengths and weaknesses as they currently exist and in an historical context. This should focus on the strengths and weaknesses of the current staff, equipment, resources and management and also include the wider issues.

- Understand the current and likely future opportunities and threats to the school and its outcomes and services. There are usually external issues which might affect the department's ability to deliver or could provide the path for future development.

- Use these first three points to put together a realistic strategy for departmental improvement. This would focus on the aims of the department but must be linked to the general aims of the school. It would also include the development of the people and a recruitment strategy for the department, where appropriate.

- Define the key performance measures by which progress can be monitored and problems identified at an early stage. This would take the approach of defining what the manager hopes to achieve and putting in place the practical measurements by which the activities can be monitored and performance evaluated.

- Identify the critical success factors which underlie the achievement of the objectives. Stated simply: 'What needs to happen before we can achieve our stated objectives?'

- Set out a realistic timetable for achievement of objectives, with intermediate steps (or short-term objectives). This should be a challenging programme otherwise managers will not devote the necessary effort. The objectives being pursued should either be central to school operations or an important new development which is intended to become central to operations.

- Set up suitable implementation and monitoring systems to ensure progress is made and / or problems are identified at an early stage. Measurement should be quick, easy and as publicly verifiable as possible.

- Implement what has been agreed. There is no point spending time on this exercise if it is not followed through. It is here that most initiatives of this sort fail.

- Maintain an open attitude to problems. If people feel that they will be blamed or publicly humiliated for the shortfalls in their achievement they will find ways to hide the true results. The initiative must be approached with a problem-solving attitude. In addition, while all managers may have their own set of objectives, the whole school should see their achievement as their common cause. There is no point in one department shining at the expense of the others.

Steps in the process
Initial review

Overview of organisation and department operations and outputs. Departmental structure and staffing. Plans and expectations for the future. Reasons for and expectations from the process.

Current situation

What does the school do well? Where could it perform better? What changes are likely over the period and what implications do these have for the whole school? What opportunities are likely to present themselves to the school? What sort of time, resources and effort would be needed to pursue these opportunities? What are the benefits for the school of pursuing these opportunities? This exercise should also be done at the level of the individual department.

Vision and direction

- How does senior management envisage school development and how does the senior teacher hope the department will develop in terms of its people, performance, equipment and outcomes to meet the school's needs?

- What are the principles by which the school and department currently operate – in particular the key attitudes and approaches that have made the school and department as successful as it has been to this point?

- What changes to these key attitudes and approaches are needed if the department and school are to develop (more of the same – and if so how realistic is this – or different)? How will these changes be achieved? What changes will be necessary in procedures, attitudes and work methods?

Physical changes needed
to achieve vision
and direction

Not just changes in technology and learning materials but also in staff numbers, training and attitudes. The size of any investment, whether monetary or otherwise, should be quantified.

Key departmental
objectives

These must be relevant to the school's objectives as defined by senior management, challenging, and achievable only with effort and measurable. At this stage, they also need a degree of flexibility. They should be over a twelve- to eighteen-month period.

Arising out of these objectives decide what factors will be critical to their achievement. It should also be possible to measure these. They will often be the steps towards achieving an objective. As well as the long-term objectives, a series of steps should be defined – short-term objectives. These should be at approximately one-monthly intervals. The assumptions that underlie their achievement should be defined. For example, if an increase in attendance depends on purchase of new computer software for monitoring then that should be stated.

Review of staffing

This includes both the existing and the planned increases or decreases in staff over the period. Stated simply: in order the achieve the objectives, what are the implications for staff development, organisation and numbers?

Any development needs identified should be based on a comparison between existing levels of knowledge and skill and those that will be needed if the organisational objectives are to be achieved. All development needs must be focused on the school's educational and, where appropriate, financial objectives and should demonstrably contribute to their achievement.

Implementation / monitoring / evaluation

Decisions as to how this will be done should be drawn up at the same time as the schedule for implementation. This cannot usually be determined until the costs are known.

At this stage a process of implementation and review needs to be put in place covering the following aspects:

- composition of the group that drives the process forward

- how to ensure agreed action actually happens

- group's decision-making powers

- resources needed (if any)

- a series of milestones with expected dates for achievement (use short-term objectives)

- key points in the programme when the process of review will focus on evaluation of effectiveness

- a clear overview of costs versus benefits and the means to measure that (costs should not just include monetary costs. In a school, people costs and time will often have more relevance. However, the financial aspects cannot be ignored).

Problems caused by other senior teachers – case studies

The following case studies seek to highlight some of the problems that can be caused by working as part of a team of senior teachers. While, generally, we welcome the support that colleagues can bring, there can be problems caused by differences of opinion, attitude and perception.

It can easily be forgotten that communication and teamwork apply at many levels in a school. This is particularly the case in large schools. Most of us recognise our membership of the team in the department to which we belong. But as a senior teacher you are also part of a management team. For the purposes of these case studies, the focus is on the management group as the team.

These case studies are usually best approached by individual review initially followed by discussion with the total management group. As always this may not be practical, but there should be discussion with at least one other person.

In some schools, how other senior teachers cope with their problems may be of interest but has little relevance as long as it does not directly affect the running of another department. Even in these schools, there are situations where co-operation and a common approach are seen to be necessary. In most working situations there is, however, a recognition for the need for common approaches to handling problems.

CASE STUDY 7.5

There have always been problems between your department and another, but these have got worse over the last few months. The two departments rely on one another and share some of the support staff. There has always been a degree of mistrust and a lack of understanding about one another's aims and objectives.

However, since the appointment of a new head to the other department, matters have become much worse. This person previously worked in that department as one of the non-management employees, and now seems to be using his position, as senior teacher, to advance his own people's point of view, at the expense of yours. In reality, each relies on the other and co-operation is much more sensible. In the past this was the case at senior teacher level, but despite genuine efforts, did not spread to the other employees.

You have tried to talk to this senior teacher about the problems he is causing but have not been successful. So far, you have resisted retaliating since you believe that would only make matters worse.

Your staff are becoming angry about what is happening. They see the others taking advantage of the situation and you are concerned that they will take matters into their own hands. Some new work has come in that would be better done if you worked together. When you approached the other senior teacher about this, he said, 'I will make my plans, you are just going to have to fit in with those.'

How would you handle the immediate situation?

What other steps could / should you take to resolve the problems in the longer term?

Analysis

This case study seeks to highlight the importance of teamwork at management level. As the case is presented, it would seem that the other senior teacher sees himself only as a member of his own department. He feels no part of and, therefore, no loyalty to the general management efforts of the school. There may be other issues involved as well, such as a lack of tact and understanding of other people's roles and problems. However, the issue is one more of clarifying roles and trying to agree and work co-operatively towards common goals. In addition, some attention to team building at management level would be beneficial.

The current situation did not arise overnight and the building of a co-operative relationship will not happen quickly either. Perhaps the real failure here was in not involving the other staff in the co-operation with the previous senior teacher. To continue to neglect this will create further problems at a future date. The details of the solution will be individual to the school but must include a means to improve the trust and working relationships between departments.

CASE STUDY 7.6

You have a totally different viewpoint to another senior teacher on virtually any issue. At times, it almost seems that if you say one thing, the other senior teacher will take up the opposing side, almost on principle. Of course, this is not actually the case, but the degree of your disagreement is profound.

The problem tends to have its most public airing at management meetings. There is a tendency for other senior teachers to side with one or other of you. You have felt at times that this has resulted in issues not being properly discussed. It just becomes a trial of strength between the two groups with the final outcome usually being some compromise which, on reflection, satisfies neither.

The problem is at its sharpest where staff are concerned. Your methods of working are so different, staff are very aware of it and use it to play one of you off against the other.

You have both been given responsibility to work on a new initiative for the school which will involve your having to work together with a group of employees. You suspect that this is the principal's way of trying to get you to improve your relationship. If some action is not taken then the initiative will probably fail because the two of you will not be able to agree.

The initiative is important for the school and for both of you. If it fails it is unlikely that either of you would be asked to participate in any important initiative again.

What steps could / should you take to resolve your differences, in order that the current project is a success?

In more general situations, what should you do, if anything, to improve your relationship with this senior teacher?

Analysis

It is unlikely that either person will shift viewpoint substantially in this situation. Interestingly, a whole school can be influenced by one articulate individual in these circumstances. However, when two such individuals hold influential positions then the scope for conflict is limitless. The lining up of other staff, with bartering-style compromises, is also very typical of this situation and not particularly helpful to good management or teamwork.

The biggest problems centre on the way it allows employees to exploit the differences. As senior teachers, you must learn to work co-operatively together and to respect one another. As long as one or both of you sees the situation as a trial of strength, matters will not improve.

You both need to agree a set of basic principles about how you are going to conduct your work together on the new initiative. If disagreements arise later these principles can be the basis on which the matter is resolved. You must also come to a working agreement with this person to support one another, at least publicly. Division between you will be exploited not only by the employees who work for you but possibly by other senior teachers.

The differences between you are not necessarily a weakness, anything you both agree to will have been argued and examined from more than one perspective. This tends to result in a better answer.

CASE STUDY 7.7

A serious problem arising out of an error at work has been dealt with by one of your senior colleagues. The matter involved a number of staff previously part of your department The staff have been blamed and in your view this is unfair. Disciplinary action has been taken – they have not been dismissed but have been given verbal or written warnings.

You believe the problem was one of poor instructions given and a lack of experience in the situation. However, the outcome has been embarrassing for the school. The real blame, in your view, lies elsewhere.

One of these staff members, with whom you have worked for some years, has approached you, informally, to ask your opinion. She believes that the punishment has been too severe and that members of management were equally to blame, but they were not punished. She believes that all the staff, including herself, have to take responsibility, but the manner in which this was done was unfair.

You are in total agreement with this person. However, you have deferred the matter by saying that you have not been involved and would like to look into it more before commenting. You are 'off the hook' short term, but you know this employee will want a proper answer from you.

In addition, you feel that by remaining silent you appear to be agreeing with the punishment and are concerned that this could have a bearing on the reaction to future incidents.

At what point is your loyalty to your colleagues superseded by your belief that what they are doing is wrong?

Has that point been reached in this case? What are your reasons for this decision?

Analysis

There is no simple answer to this question. The case study seeks to highlight the point at which you feel that you cannot automatically support the actions of another senior teacher. Clearly there will be differences in approach between senior teachers. In most cases, however, you would still be able to support the action of another senior teacher even though you would not do that yourself.

At what the point does that break down? What would you do in those circumstances?

The case study does not give enough detail to be able to give a definitive answer in this case. Its importance is in the discussion around the general principle and in establishing an accepted procedure in these types of cases. It can only genuinely be resolved through management group decisions. However, any disagreements you have with other senior teachers should be aired either with them directly or with more senior management. It is not good practice to criticise other senior teachers outside the management team. That simply makes you all look foolish.

CASE STUDY 7.8

One member of the senior staff of the school seems to be totally at odds with the entire approach to the work of the rest of management. It is not just that she disagrees with the handling of specific incidents, which you all do, it is the whole philosophy and approach.

For example, in disciplinary matters, she feels that the emphasis is too much on punishment and not enough on encouraging right attitudes and prevention. While the rest of you do not believe that your policies and procedures are aimed that way, nothing you do seems to satisfy this senior teacher.

She is an experienced and highly capable member of staff. There is no question about her capabilities, but she seems to see the world differently from the rest of you. Whenever she expresses her concerns at management meetings, or elsewhere in public, they are listened to. In private, however, they tend to be dismissed or, sometimes, made the butt of humour by other staff. This person is seen as someone who holds rather eccentric and impractical views.

These differences cause other problems from time to time. For example, she is often expected to support a particular action that she totally disagrees with. This teacher would not 'break ranks' publicly with the rest of you but others know that she does not believe in what she is doing.

The principal has given this person a fair hearing. She has expressed some sympathy for this senior teacher's views but equally made clear that they are not hers. While she has also made it clear that it is good to have different views, it is unlikely that this senior teacher will be able to influence school policy in the foreseeable future.

How could you reconcile the differences between this teacher and the rest?

Analysis

This case study seeks to extend some of the issues raised in Case Study 7.6. In this situation, however, the differences seem to be irreconcilable. While attitudes and approaches can change it seems unlikely that this senior teacher will ever be able to give support to the school's policies. In addition, it would seem that she is not influencing management policy in the way that would be expected.

The most obvious answer is for her to leave and find a post in an school with a philosophy closer to her own. In practical terms this may not be an option. So what she must try to do is work within the system.

Some managers in these circumstances would not directly challenge the status quo but seek to subvert it in any way they can. This is a destructive approach. It is at odds with the entire thrust of this book, which is to get commitment from as wide a range of people as possible and emphasise teamwork as the way to make progress.

Perhaps the real challenge in this case study rests with the other senior staff and particularly the principal. It is their ability to accommodate at least some of the views of this individual that will be the measure of the strength of the management team. If the odd one out can at least be listened to and her views accepted as genuine, this is a step in the right direction. It is also, of course, a mutual affair.

A school's policy, on any issue, must give clear structure and direction. Every point will not be given equal place. However, it is important that everyone has the opportunity to express a viewpoint without being ridiculed.

Staff handling case studies

The following case studies seek to highlight those staff handling situations where the individual is difficult to influence or the problem defies solution. Simple handling strategies would seldom be enough in such cases although these do have their place with regards to the immediate situation. In most cases like this the person is performing as expected by the 'letter of the law' but is still causing serious problems for those managing him.

The discussion of these case studies is best done in small groups initially, rather than individually. The main focus for discussion is often on the exceptional nature of the cases. These cases seek to push your policies and procedures for managing to the limit. Where you do decide to make an exception, it is important to consider the effect this is likely to have on policies and procedures. It is important that an exception is precisely that and does not become the start of a trend.

In most of the cases studies in this section there is no immediate solution as such, and analysis given, therefore, seeks to highlight the issues. Arguably, in some cases, the 'right answer' is to continue to do things in the proper manner and remain vigilant for opportunities to improve matters. In virtually all the cases, there is a disciplinary and motivational aspect and the 'right answer' will usually be some balance of these two.

CASE STUDY 7.9

Since starting with the school this member of staff has been a problem. He is deeply unpopular with the entire staff, he is opinionated, arrogant and at times offensive in the way he expresses himself. This person has an opinion about how everyone else should do their job and it is usually unflattering to the others involved. Often there is a degree of truth in what he says but it is also often completely unfair to the people concerned.

This person is not usually asked for his views and is not in a management role. However, that has never been a barrier to the expression of an opinion by this staff member. There are few who have escaped his criticism over the time he has been employed.

Otherwise, this person's work is excellent. He has an appetite for work that you have seldom seen from anyone else and his work is of good quality. He has a tendency to be very precise about how things are done and will always insist on having the best of everything.

It is very probable that at least some of the disagreements centre around this attitude. This person will take books, resources and equipment whether or not anyone else needs them to complete his work.

You are concerned that the level of animosity from the rest of the staff is rising and complaints are becoming more frequent. The staff member is not a difficult person for management to deal with. You do believe, however, that there will be further problems with the other employees. Some of the recent arguments have been quite heated. There has however, never been an incident that could be termed disciplinary in nature.

How could this situation best be handled?

Analysis

The issue of employees who are good at their job not being able to get on together is a common one. However, in this situation such a large group is involved that it takes on a different dimension. A school wide- or department-focused initiative on teamwork could be useful. It is unlikely, however, to solve the underlying problem but it may make it tolerable within the working situation. Behaviour like this does not occur without reason. There is a range of possibilities, but they are likely to lie outside the work place.

If this employee could be given a role which suits his capabilities, but minimises his need for contact with the others, that could help or could simply emphasise his 'differentness'. Another possibility is to try to influence others to develop a better relationship with the person. Then his acceptability to the rest will rise.

CASE STUDY 7.10

The employee in question is your best staff member, if enthusiasm, willingness and speed were the only important issues. She is always willing and works very hard but is also extremely careless. There have been occasions when her lack of attention to detail has resulted in serious problems and for this she has been reprimanded. However, in most circumstances, this is not a problem. She is aware of the limits of what is acceptable and stays just within them.

However, you are concerned at the problems this person leaves in her wake. As her manager you have suffered particularly with regards to this. You have spoken to her about it several times. She is always very sorry, always promises that it will not happen again and always tries extremely hard. Then during some crisis or emergency the standards slip again and you are back to how it was before.

In addition, you have more junior staff members who see what this person does, and does not do, and who then copy her. You are now convinced that you will not be able to raise overall standards in the department unless this person's problems are tackled. Equally, you believe that you are unlikely to make any long-term difference to the way this person works.

How could you best handle this problem?

Analysis

It is always very difficult to reprimand someone who is so hard-working and willing. Furthermore, you will often find that this type of behaviour has been encouraged and sometimes rewarded and praised by management over a number of years. To turn from this to a disciplinary approach would usually be seen as inappropriate (particularly if you believe that the school might value this person and her approach again).

The most effective approach in this situation is to involve this person in setting and, more important, monitoring the standards of work. The biggest problem with this approach is getting the employee to stop doing and start looking at how things should be done. Involvement in monitoring the quality of work at a general level in the school could be particularly effective.

Case study 7.11

Clare is in the department you took responsibility for only six months ago. The last six months have been very hectic for you. There have been endless problems and changes and you have not had the time to get to know your staff in the way you would like.

Clare has come to your attention mainly through her absences. She has been missing a great deal since you started. These absences have varied in length from one or two days to up to two weeks. All absences have been properly certificated, according to school procedures. Doctor's certificates indicate a series of minor illnesses which do not seem to have any pattern.

You enquire about Clare's previous record and it would seem that this has been a fairly common pattern in the past. No formal steps have been taken. Some feel that Clare is very good at judging just how much she will get away with and the attendance pattern will match that. This is borne out by the facts. Clare has had a lot of absence over a long period and no action has been taken. She was referred once to the school's doctor. This coincided with a period of good attendance and the doctor reported that there were no medical problems. There have been no major absences, rather a continuous series of minor illnesses.

You have tried to see Clare several times, but so far have not spoken to her. The absences and the pressure of work you have been under have made this difficult. Clare knows the procedures in detail, by all accounts, and will ensure that you will not be able to take any action against her. You will need to proceed with care.

How could you best handle this situation?

Analysis

This situation should, arguably, never have arisen and can be easily dealt with through the school's absence and disciplinary procedures. However, it is seldom as simple as that. You could be dealing with someone who knows the rules and procedures probably better than you, and will seek to exploit them to the full. You could also be dealing with a very real and genuine sickness and one that could be work related.

Your initial steps should all be investigatory. Why is this person off so much? Is there any pattern to the absences? Are the absences due to work-related illness? What exactly is the extent and pattern of the absences and how long has this been going on? In addition, you must find a way to see this person and discuss the problem with her in an open manner.

The outcome of this type of problem is difficult to predict but it will almost certainly require close monitoring. It is easy, in a case like this, to pre-judge the issue. Be careful that you have genuine evidence for any steps you take. Look for hard evidence, do not rely on gossip and uninformed opinion.

CASE STUDY 7.12

Martin is a very difficult person to get on with. He will question your every instruction or suggestion, either to your face, or with other teachers when you are not present. Martin believes that he should have got a senior teacher's job but was prevented from doing so by fear and jealousy among some of the existing senior teachers, because he would 'show them up'.

In fact, his work and results are good but no better than that of many other teachers. In terms of interpersonal skills, you believe that Martin will never be capable of doing a management job and this is almost certainly one of the reasons why he has never been offered one.

In day-to-day work you do not have any complaints about Martin. However, this tendency to question everything does pose problems. It is very difficult to try anything new. He will condemn the proposal immediately, whatever source it comes from. If you insist, he will comply with bad grace and highlight any problems that arise. Inevitably, there will be teething problems and minor changes. Martin will point to these as proof that you had not thought through your ideas to start with. He has a selective memory about events.

Other employees are not normally affected by his negativity. However, he will exploit any concerns of other employees, raise unnecessary fears about even the simplest proposed change and misinterpret the motives of management.

You have tried to involve him in changes. This has not worked – he is so negative and difficult to deal with that the other staff become angry at his obstruction. In the end, you have had to make decisions which he did not agree with or abandon the proposed change.

You are fed up with his behaviour. There are a number of planned changes about to happen in your department. Martin has already spoken of his opposition to them and is starting to voice groundless concerns about the effect they will have on the numbers employed. In fact, the changes should slightly increase the numbers needed.

However, if you do not take action the other employees will start to listen to him and this will make the changes much more difficult to implement. It is important that you have their goodwill and co-operation.

How could this situation be best handled?

Analysis

This case study has elements in common with many others. The person concerned is good at his job but he is causing other problems which are affecting your ability to do your job.

In the short term you could stop this person by warning him of the consequences of going against you. However, you might just drive the problem 'underground'. It would be better if this person could feel part of the decision-making process and committed to what the team was trying to do.

Realistically, this is unlikely in the foreseeable future with this person. Your best hope of improvement may lie in the attitudes of other team members. It is important to give this person his say and place in any discussions but you may have to accept that you are unlikely to change his attitudes. It may be a problem that has to be coped with in the short to medium term. Ensure that your communication with other staff is accurate, clear and frequent.

Mentoring skills

The concept of mentoring has become more popular in recent years and has come about as a result of a recognition that formal training and development programmes focus on approaches, techniques and principles but in any organisation there will be informal approaches and knowledge which will be invaluable to any member of staff.

As we understand the concept now it has much in common with the old notion of apprenticeship. The new member of staff is assigned to a more experienced and skilled person who is willing to share knowledge. The person learns by working closely with this person.

In schools the concept has been used in recent years with new members of teaching staff in particular. However, it undoubtedly has applications with any job or role. In some schools it has been extended to pupils. There are a number of variations on this. A common one relates to pupils who have learning or behaviour problems. They are assigned to an older pupil who reviews their work and helps them appropriately.

The mentoring role is a practical one and, when applied to a staff situation, it is the new staff member who will drive the process and be responsible for her own development. The role of the mentor is to act as a sounding board and give advice and guidance. Senior teachers and heads of departments are probably the two most popular choices for this role. However, any person who has the following characteristics would make a suitable mentor:

- experience of the school

- reasonable knowledge of the job of the person being mentored

- good interpersonal skills

- sympathy to the approaches being suggested

- willingness to take on the role.

The last characteristic is probably the most important. If the person wants to take on the role, time will be made to review and discuss the work done by the person being mentored (for ease of expression, we shall refer to this person as the 'participant'). Otherwise, there will always be good reasons why time cannot be found or meetings have to be cancelled.

While there is no requirement for a great deal of administration, it is useful if brief records are kept of these meetings. A form is suggested to record briefly the topics covered and the actions the participant agrees to take before the next meeting. Table 7.1 shows a typical such form.

The role of the mentor is to provide a focus for the participant's efforts, to be a sounding board, to discuss areas of concern and to encourage and support the participant. It is not to do the work for the person. It would normally be better if the mentor had some knowledge of the likely areas of concern or discussion prior to the meeting. However, that should not act as a barrier to a meeting taking place.

It is difficult to give precise advice about how often the mentor and participant should meet. The simple answer is as often as is necessary and useful. Normally, this will be more often in the first weeks and months of the participant's employment. The regular contact with and expectations of the mentor can help maintain this motivation. A regular meeting time can be useful.

Some organisations have found it useful to draw up a mentoring contract between participant and mentor, in which each person's responsibilities and expectations are defined. This ensures that both remain realistic about what is expected from the other. A sample contract can be found in Table 7.2. This provides guidance only, and the actual contents must remain a matter for agreement between participant and mentor.

The length of time that mentoring should continue for is a matter for the individual school. It has been normal for it to last for either one or two years. What is important is that it has a definite course to run, which both mentor and participant understand, and it can be shortened or lengthened by agreement. The expectations of both sides should be clear from the start. Many new employees assume that the mentor will actually do work for them. Mentoring is about helping the other person do things for themselves so that needs to be spelt out clearly from the outset. The mentor also needs to guard against solving the participant's problems. This will not help their long-term on-the-job learning.

Table 7.1. Sample mentoring programme record sheet

MEETINGS RECORD

PARTICIPANT _____ MENTOR _____

DATE _____ TIME _____

TOPICS / ISSUES DISCUSSED

1

2

3

4

5

AGREED ACTIONS

1

2

3

4

5

DATE OF NEXT MEETING _____

Table 7.2. Sample mentoring agreement

MENTORING AGREEMENT

PARTICIPANT _____ MENTOR _____

THE FOLLOWING SETS OUT THE ROLES AND RESPONSIBILITIES OF THE PERSON PARTICIPATING IN THE MENTORING PROGRAMME AND THE PERSON GIVING HIM / HER HELP AND SUPPORT ON BEHALF OF THE SCHOOL.

Participant's responsibilities:

1 To demonstrate interest and motivation for the job and for the process of mentoring. To complete any tasks or actions agreed at mentoring meetings within the timescale set out.

2 To give reasonable notice of an inability to attend mentoring meetings or of not having completed work for meetings.

3 To maintain interest in the process of mentoring by committing personal and working time to it, which will average _____ hours per week, in total, over a period of _____ years. If this should change the participant will agree changes in the amount per week and the duration of the mentoring programme as necessary.

4 To be on time for meetings and ensure that the mentor's time is not wasted by your actions or failure to take action.

5 To be willing openly to discuss work-related or other problems effecting your work.

6 To use those giving support within the organisation, but to be reasonable in the demands placed on their time.

Mentor's responsibilities:

1 To provide regular (usually monthly) support meetings and training sessions for the participant. To organise working time so that the participant can be free to attend meetings and any other associated activities.

2 To demonstrate an interest in the programme through ensuring the participant is kept informed of arrangements and changes to them, providing reasonable open access to the participant. To give support and guidance to the participant.

3 To agree with the participant the dates and times of regular meetings.

4 To meet reasonable requests for other support and help, wherever possible.

5 To give reasonable notice of changes in arrangements.

Any other responsibilities:

1

2

3

SIGNED _____   _____
                          PARTICIPANT   MENTOR

DATE _____

Development of the mentoring relationship

While mentoring tends to be a very individual process, the following gives an overview of how a mentoring relationship might develop.

Initial contact

Discussion of expectations, likely content of meetings and other details relating to the process. Both mentor and participant would normally outline their working and educational background and brief personal details. The mentor would outline the structure of the school and reporting arrangements and management structure and style as it currently exists, agreement on regularity, location and duration of meetings. Agreement on the records which need to be kept (usually the mentor completes the first record and the participant the rest) and how quickly they will be returned to the other person. The mentoring agreement is usually (modified and) signed at this meeting.

Analysis of current situation

Focusing initially on the personal strengths and weaknesses of the participant (ensuring that weaknesses are used constructively as development issues). The mentor and participant should agree what help, support and development opportunities the participant will need. These will often be the responsibility of the mentor to either deliver or source but the participant should be given responsibility for as much of this as possible, as early as possible.

Direction

It is useful at an early stage to try to define where it is hoped the mentoring process will lead. What differences will be expected in the knowledge, skills and confidence of the participant by the end of the process.

First steps

In any process of change, the first steps are extremely important in defining expectations and in getting momentum going. This will usually involve setting out specific actions which must be taken before the next meeting. These should be of sufficient magnitude to make the process worthwhile and achievable in order to build confidence.

Arising out of these actions will be factors critical to their achievement. It should also be possible to measure these. They will often be steps towards achieving a goal or objective. The mentor's role will be to ensure that the actions meet the criteria defined.

Maintaining progress

The participant discusses any problems in meeting the agreed actions and indeed problems of any sort that are job related. The mentor gives direct advice and support where needed. However, the aim of mentoring is to gradually withdraw direct support so that the mentor eventually acts only as a sounding board, listening, reflecting comments, asking questions, defining vague areas and helping the participant to clarify what needs to be done.

Ongoing development needs would continue to be identified from discussions, problems and an understanding of likely future needs within the school which the mentor would need.

Monitoring and evaluation

Where appropriate, the mentor would observe the participant at work and review performance, giving direct feedback and advice.

Monitoring and evaluating the process will form the content of the bulk of meetings after the initial three or four. It tends to take the format of:

- review of progress against actions decided at last meeting

- discussion on issues arising and reasons for any failure to complete actions

- review of current situation against final goals / objectives for the programme

- discussion of any other problems which the participant has

- feedback from mentor on the participant's work and progress

- agreement on actions needed for next meeting (including an allocation of responsibility for taking action)

- date, time and location of next meeting agreed.

Conclusion of mentoring process

Agree how and when the process will end and any follow-up contact.